THE BOOK OF JEWISH SACRED PRACTICES

CLAL's Guide to Everyday & Holiday Rituals & Blessings

Edited by
Rabbi Irwin Kula and Vanessa L. Ochs, Ph.D.

JEWISH LIGHTS Publishing
Woodstock, Vermont

The Book of Jewish Sacred Practices:
CLAL's Guide to Everyday & Holiday Rituals & Blessings

© 2001 by CLAL

CLAL is The National Jewish Center for Learning and Leadership.

For information regarding permission to reprint material from this book, please mail or fax your request in writing to Jewish Lights Publishing, Permissions Department, at the address / fax number listed below.

Library of Congress Cataloging-in-Publication Data
The Book of Jewish sacred practices : CLAL's guide to everyday & holiday rituals & blessings / edited by Irwin Kula and Vanessa Ochs.
    p. cm.
ISBN 1–58023–152–7 (Paperback)
1. Judaism—Prayer-books and devotions. 2. Jewish way of life. 3. Judaism—Customs and practices. 4. Jewish meditations. 5. Benediction—Judaism. 6. Benedictions. I. Kula, Irwin.
    II. Ochs, Vanessa L.
BM665 .K85 2001
296.4–dc21

2001002553

10 9 8 7 6 5 4 3 2 1

Manufactured in Canada

Cover art: *Exodus* (© 2000) was painted by Michael Bogdanow, an artist, lawyer and musician living in Lexington, Massachusetts. It is inspired by the Passover seder in which it is said that "in each generation, every one of us must feel that he, that she, has personally gone out of Egypt." Bogdanow states that "it reflects every human's crossing of every Red Sea throughout all time." The original is an acrylic painting on canvas and is part of the artist's "Visions of Torah" series of contemporary, spiritual paintings and reproductions inspired by Judaic texts.

Published by Jewish Lights Publishing
A Division of LongHill Partners, Inc.
Sunset Farm Offices, Route 4, P.O. Box 237
Woodstock, VT 05091
Tel: (802) 457-4000   Fax: (802) 457-40004

www.jewishlights.com

CONTENTS

PARENTS AND CHILDREN

RELATIONSHIPS

SPECIAL MOMENTS

HEALING

LIFE AND DEATH

LEARNING

LEADERSHIP AND COMMUNAL LIFE

ISRAEL

TZEDAKAH

HOLY DAYS

ACKNOWLEDGMENTS

This book has been the effort of the entire CLAL faculty, which
represents all denominations of Judaism. It exemplifies CLAL's
mission to help build vital Jewish communities in the twenty-first
century that are pluralist and inclusive, to develop new forms of
Jewish thought and practice, to stimulate volunteer and professional
leaders to imagine the Jewish future, and to enhance Jewish participation in civic and spiritual life.

Special thanks to CLAL faculty and administrative staff—project
manager Janet R. Kirchheimer, who oversaw all aspects of the book;
Hannah Gastfreund, who typed and laid out the entire manuscript; and
Ruth Bregman and Dr. David Kraemer for their technical assistance.

Rabbi Irwin Kula and Dr. Vanessa L. Ochs envisioned the concept and orchestrated the development of the book, and we are
deeply appreciative of Vanessa Ochs's expertise in editing.

We are also grateful to CLAL's many students and participants
who played an important role in the evolution of these sacred
practices and rituals that link our heritage with contemporary life,
renewing the old and sanctifying the new.

Donna M. Rosenthal
Executive Vice Chairman

ABOUT THE
CONTRIBUTORS

Rabbi Judith Z. Abrams, Ph.D., is a CLAL Associate. She was ordained at the Hebrew Union College and received her Ph.D. in Rabbinic Literature from Baltimore Hebrew University.

Rabbi Tsvi Blanchard, Ph.D., is Director of Organizational Development at CLAL. He was ordained at the St. Louis Rabbinical College and received his Ph.D. in Psychology from St. Louis University and his Ph.D. in Philosophy from Washington University.

Rabbi Daniel Silberman Brenner is a Senior Teaching Fellow at CLAL. He received his M.A. in Hebrew Letters and his ordination from the Reconstructionist Rabbinical College.

Shari Cohen, Ph.D., is a Senior Fellow at CLAL. She received her Ph.D. in Political Science from the University of California, Berkeley.

David M. Elcott, Ph.D., formerly Academic Vice President at CLAL, received his Ph.D. in Modern Jewish History from Columbia University.

Rabbi Niles E. Goldstein, formerly a CLAL Steinhardt Senior Fellow, received his M.A. from and was ordained at Hebrew Union College.

Michael Gottsegen, Ph.D., is Director of Internet Programs at CLAL. He received his Ph.D. in Political Theory from Columbia University and is completing his Ph.D. in Religion at Harvard University.

Rabbi Irving (Yitz) Greenberg, Ph.D., is President Emeritus and co-founder of CLAL. He received ordination from Beth Joseph Rabbinical Seminary and his Ph.D. in History from Harvard University.

Rabbi Steven Greenberg is a Senior Teaching Fellow at CLAL. He received his rabbinical ordination from Rabbi Isaac Elchanan Theological Seminary of Yeshiva University.

Rabbi Brad Hirschfield is Director of Leadership and Communities at CLAL. He received ordination from the Institute of Traditional Judaism and his M.A. and M.Phil. in Ancient Jewish History from the Jewish Theological Seminary.

Janet R. Kirchheimer is Director of Community Development and Assistant to the President of CLAL. She received her B.S. in Business Administration from Central Connecticut State College.

David Kraemer, Ph.D., is a CLAL Associate. He received his M.A. and Ph.D. in Talmud and Rabbinics from the Jewish Theological Seminary.

Rabbi Jennifer E. Krause is a CLAL Associate. She received her M.A. in Hebrew Literature from and was ordained at Hebrew Union College.

Rabbi Irwin Kula is President of CLAL. He received his B.H.L., his M.A. in Rabbinics, and his ordination from the Jewish Theological Seminary.

Rabbi Benay Lappe was a CLAL Spielberg Fellow and is a CLAL Associate. She received an M.A. in Rabbinic Literature and ordination from the Jewish Theological Seminary.

Rabbi Natan Margalit was a CLAL Steinhardt Fellow. He was ordained at the Jerusalem Orthodox Seminary.

Rabbi David Nelson, Ph.D., is a Senior CLAL Associate. He received his ordination from Hebrew Union College and his Ph.D. in Midrash from New York University.

Vanessa L. Ochs, Ph.D., is a Senior CLAL Associate. She received her Ph.D. in the Anthropology of Religion from Drew University.

Rabbi Rachel T. Sabath is a CLAL Associate. She was ordained at Hebrew Union College. She is completing a Ph.D. in Jewish Philosophy from the Jewish Theological Seminary.

Robert Rabinowitz, Ph.D., is a Senior Fellow at CLAL. He received his Ph.D. in Philosophy from London University.

Andrew Silow-Carroll was a CLAL Spielberg Fellow. He received his B.A. in English from the State University of New York at Albany.

Rabbi Lawrence Troster was a CLAL Steinhardt Fellow. He received his M.A. and his rabbinic ordination from the Jewish Theological Seminary.

PREFACE

Despite all of our material accomplishments and the valued comfort and security they provide, we sense something lacking within our hearts and in the way we connect to others. Our busy and harried lives often keep us from taking the time to understand, appreciate, and embrace the experiences that pass us by. We miss much of our lives and become strangers to ourselves, not knowing our inner world—who and what we really are. So we hunger for something, some way, some words or actions that will sustain us.

This book responds to the needs of our inner lives. The rituals, blessings, and meditations within provide a means to unveil the deeper significance of our life experiences, tools for awakening and self-transformation. What we get from each moment ultimately depends on the attention *(kavanah)* we give to those moments, and the quality of our experience reflects the quality of our awareness. These practices invite us to greater awareness, making us more present to catch the subtleties of our experience. With this awareness comes the ability to know ourselves more clearly, to serve more joyfully, and to love others more deeply—Torah, *avodah*, *gemilut chasadim*. Sometimes, like Jacob, we may suddenly recognize that "God is in this place, and I did not know it."

In this book, we have attempted to "renew the old" by offering new in-sights into ancient traditions that may have become routine. We have also tried to "sanctify the new" by providing ways to bring awareness of the beauty and potential that are hidden within experiences not yet addressed by Jewish tradition. We use Jewish metaphors and symbols not because they are necessarily better or more true than those of other traditions, but because of our love for them. We are among the fortunate in our generation for whom Jewish wisdom works to awaken within us the deeper awareness and dimension of our lives. This wisdom is our inheritance, not our possession. Therefore, we hope that whatever one's religious identity, these practices will enhance life, for they require no specific religious beliefs nor do they require giving up any specific religious beliefs. This book is much more concerned with learning and living than with believing. All that is necessary is a willingness to experiment. Each page is meant not only to be read but to be a catalyst for both awareness and action.

We hope that these rituals, blessings, and meditations will help you to be kinder and more hopeful, more open and forgiving, more grateful and generous, more joyful and humble, more playful and just. The Jewish wisdom tradition teaches us to "choose life"; if, even in a small way, this book helps you to feel more alive and more human, then the dreams of our ancestors to sanctify life will be fulfilled.

Irwin Kula
Editor

INTRODUCTION

RENEW THE OLD, SANCTIFY THE NEW

At CLAL—The National Jewish Center for Learning and
Leadership, we are often asked to help people locate or develop
meditations, rituals, blessings, and meaningful teachings to mark
important events in their lives. They might be hoping to conceive
a child, or they're starting a new job, or they've just quit smoking,
or they're retiring. They might be taking on a volunteer role in
the community, or they might want to bless their children on the
Sabbath or do some spiritual preparation for the High Holidays.
They want to acknowledge a whole range of life experiences, some
that are obviously Jewish in nature and some that seem less so.
As we have discovered, and as our sages have long known, there
is no experience in the life of a Jew that cannot be marked in
Jewish ways. There are times when the available Jewish rituals just
don't seem to fit well enough to use, and we need to adapt them.
There are also times when there really isn't an obvious Jewish way
to mark some of the events of our lives, and we work together to
develop new rituals that are deeply based in tradition.

We, as rabbis and Jewish scholars, bring our collective expertise
in sacred Jewish texts and traditions. We have searched through
ancient and contemporary Jewish practices and liturgies, and we
have experimented in bringing fresh Jewish practices to Jewish
communities across the country for more than twenty-five years.
The people who approach us, seeking our assistance, bring to the
table the very personal ways they find meaning in their own lives.
They know why it's so important to them to mark this event in a

Jewish way. They know what kind of personal and spiritual work they hope this ritual might accomplish. They may even know which Jewish texts and symbols can speak meaningfully to them, so that this moment of their lives can be connected to the past and linked to the future.

The book you hold in your hands is the result of the kinds of rituals we have sculpted together over the years.

It is not a prayer book or even a compendium of obligatory Jewish rituals. Rather, it is a resource for all to use creatively. The meditations, rituals, blessings, and meaningful Jewish teachings we have discovered, created, and assembled are the result of hundreds of hours of collaborative work carried out by the CLAL faculty, fellows, and associates. For CLAL, this resource is the beginning of a much larger process of CLAL's Jewish resource development, in which we will be developing and presenting resources for many more events in people's lives that they are experiencing as Jews and wish to mark as Jews.

As we created this collection, we were guided by considerations to which we are deeply committed:

- We believe that our meditations, rituals, blessings, and teachings can connect us to Jewish traditions and resonate strongly with our everyday personal experiences.

- When we speak of God, we believe that we should draw from a wide range of images that feel real and inspirational to us.

- There are many ways in which to experience a sacred presence, and they all take work. If we believe that it is possible to encounter God or be open to God's encountering us, we must attend to how this happens; we need to take the time to ready ourselves and prepare our sacred space.

- Because of our commitment to the sacred plurality of Jews everywhere, the resources we offer in this compendium are culturally inclusive, respecting the ethnic, geographic, and religious diversity of Jews and the communities in which we live. We trust that these resources are sensitive to both women and men of different ages. They were created so that anyone can use them; you don't need a rabbi or other Jewish expert. If we have been successful, they will help people to live richer Jewish lives.

HOW TO USE THIS BOOK

Before deciding if you will try a Jewish practice as we have presented it as a script or if you prefer to adapt it significantly to fit your own needs as a springboard, you'll want to study the resources we have provided. You'll notice that for each life event, we provide a meditation, ritual, blessing, and a selection of relevant Jewish teachings.

If you want to perform a ritual with other people, you'll need to decide whom to invite. Let them know just why their presence is important. They'll feel more comfortable if you explain what will happen and what's expected of them. If you will not be the sole leader of the ceremony, let others know beforehand what you will be asking them to prepare, do, or say. When others can help you prepare in some way or participate, they will feel more involved.

IF YOU CHOOSE TO USE THIS BOOK AS A SCRIPT

1. Focus your concentration and place other concerns and distractions you can anticipate aside. Begin by dwelling on the meditation, reading it to yourself or reciting it quietly as many times as you wish. Make copies for everyone you've invited to participate. A meditation, or *kavanah*, is a classic Jewish way of preparing ourselves for a sacred moment. It quiets us, aligns us, and focuses our concentration. It enables us to become more attuned to the Divine Presence.

2. Perform the ritual. You'll see that the rituals are, in large part, traditional Jewish practices that are familiar to many and can be performed comfortably and easily.

3. Speak the blessing aloud after the ritual is performed. (What exactly is a blessing? Marcia Falk has taught that for a Jew, blessings are "the practice of marking occasions—both ordinary and extraordinary ones—with special speech-acts that increase our

awareness of our actions.") You'll see that the blessings we've presented are familiar and are drawn from the traditional Jewish liturgical vocabulary of blessing as found in the Torah, the Talmud, and the prayer book. When we have adapted ancient blessings for modern usage, we have tried to stay rooted in their original meanings and sentiments.

4. Study the teachings, as they will add depth to the event you are marking. You may wish to study them as part of your own preparation, or you may choose to copy them and study the texts in pairs or as a group as part of your ceremony.

IF YOU CHOOSE TO USE THIS BOOK AS A SPRINGBOARD

Let the meditations, rituals, blessings, and teachings be your sources of inspiration, points of departure as you develop your own Jewish responses to the events of your life. Let the meditations we've created help you to uncover your own meditations; and let our rituals, blessings, and teachings do likewise and spur you on with confidence and creativity.

QUESTIONS YOU MAY HAVE

WILL THESE RESOURCES "WORK" FOR ME?

We hope many of these rituals will provide you with enough guidance to start out. We know that some resources may not feel quite right to you, and we hope you will be as comfortable with this initial feeling of discomfort as we are. Either you will find ways to adapt the ritual or you will pass, saying, "This is not for me, at least not right now." One advantage of a tradition as old and rich as ours is the huge variety of available Jewish responses. For instance, for generations Jews lit oil lamps on the Sabbath, and some continue to do so. However, most of us now light Sabbath candles, and that feels right to us (so right that we might find it hard to imagine beginning the Sabbath without lighting white candles!). We know we can experiment until we discover sacred Jewish expressions that fit our situation, the age we live in, the time of our lives, and our temperaments.

ARE THE RESOURCES "AUTHENTICALLY JEWISH"?

Our sturdy Jewish tradition allows us freedom to experiment, innovate, and be expressive in Jewish language. Jews have always developed liturgical and ritual responses to their lives; think of the patriarch Jacob, who, after his night spent encountering an angel, gathered together a pile of rocks and called the place he was in "Bet El"—God's house. Some innovations take hold and are widely adopted. For instance, Jews did not always use Chanukah menorahs, spice boxes, or Purim groggers. We did not always celebrate Israel's Independence Day with parades or by singing "Hatikvah." It's hard to imagine, but Jews did not always use the wedding *chuppah* or celebrate weddings inside synagogues. Although the wedding *chuppah* in a synagogue is now considered the definitive symbol of a Jewish wedding, the practice was inspired by churches in medieval Europe. Other Jewish innovations "work" for a while and then seem to fade away or become transformed: *kapporas* comes to mind, the ritual of twirling fowl over one's head before Yom Kippur to remove one's sins. While some of our great-grandparents may have observed this ritual, few of us have live fowl out on our decks or balconies, and even if we did, we probably wouldn't feel right twirling them over our heads. Thus, *kapporas* has been replaced with the twirling of money for *tzedakah* wrapped in a handkerchief or transformed altogether into the "Kol Nidrei Appeal."

WHO DETERMINES WHAT GETS INCORPORATED AND WHAT FALLS AWAY?

Our wise men and women have taught: "*Lo bashamayim hi*"— the decision is not made by God in heaven. It is we—the living, breathing Jewish community—who decide. In our generation, the Jewish community has affirmed such practices as the observance of Yom Ha'atzma'ut, the singing of "Hatikvah," the bat mitzvah, naming ceremonies for daughters, and healing services.

HOW IS THE NAME OF GOD BEING USED?

You will see that we have spelled out the name of God in transliteration just as it is pronounced because we want people who do not read Hebrew easily to be able to say the blessings correctly. As Rabbi Irving (Yitz) Greenberg teaches, it is permissible to use English and transliterated renditions of the name of God, for neither is the actual name of God. In accordance with Jewish tradition, we do not print the name of God in Hebrew. This choice reflects CLAL's efforts to be as sensitive as possible to different religious sensibilities and practices as we broadly explore the ways that Judaism can be maximally expansive.

Some of the new blessings we have created include the name of God. If it makes you more comfortable, you could certainly say the blessing without including the name of God.

Because God's name is present in this book, the book has a special status and should be treated with the same care as a Bible or prayer book. Rabbi Tsvi Blanchard explains that if you need to discard this book, you should bring it to a synagogue that has a "*shemot* box," a special holder of sacred books and papers with God's name that will be treated in a most respectful way.

Vanessa L. Ochs
Editor

EVERYDAY LIFE

WAKING UP

As soon as I sit up in bed and see the light through the windows, I am suddenly aware I'm alive and a new day has begun. Then I say to myself something like this: "Thank you, God. I know You're still out there doing Your thing, because here I am again doing my thing, thanks to You." That's my version of the *Modeh Ani* prayer, which appears in my *siddur* as: "I render thanks unto Thee, everlasting King, who has mercifully restored my soul within me; Thy faithfulness is beyond measure."

קוּמִי!

Kumi!

Arise!

As I continue my morning ritual, I do my own riffs on the traditional morning prayers. As I put on my glasses, I say: "Whoa! I can see again!" for "Blessed art Thou...who openest the eyes of the blind." As I pull my body out of bed: "I'm standing on my feet. Thank You!" for "Blessed art Thou ...who raisest up those who are bowed down." As I dress: "Clean, fresh clothes!" for "Blessed art Thou...who clothest the naked."

Meditation

מוֹדָה אֲנִי לְפָנֶיךָ.

Modeh ani l'fanekha.

Thank You, God, for waking me up and giving me another day.

Ritual

After waking and saying your own version of *Modeh Ani*, pause, even if it's only for a few seconds, to register: it really is a miracle to be alive for this new day! It doesn't really matter what language you use, or whether you say it out loud or to yourself. Just stop and notice: I'm awake, I can see, I'm getting up, I'm washing, I'm dressing. Be aware of the feelings that come as you make these observations. It is these feelings that generated the traditional prayers in the first place.

Blessing

With every part of my being I praise the One who is clothed in splendor and majesty, wrapped in light as in a garment, unfolding the heavens like a curtain.

Teaching

How long will you lie there, lazybones? When will you wake from your sleep? A bit more sleep, a bit more slumber, a bit more hugging yourself in bed.

(Proverbs 6:9–10)

This assignment originated from the Baal Shem Tov's advice that every Jew should make 100 blessings a day. Did they have to be in Hebrew? Did they have to be only for Jewish things? I explained to the class that the idea of the homework was to notice all the ways in which their lives were blessed and that making 100 blessings would be so challenging that they would not have any energy to notice anything but blessing.

(Johanna J. Singer, "100 Blessings a Day," in Traditions *by Sarah Shendelman and Avram Davis)*

PRAYING FOR WHAT WE NEED

In theory, praying for what we need should be easy. Who knows better what we need than we do? However, we wonder: is it okay to ask for the very private things that are important to us? Should we be distinguishing between what we *want* and what we *need*? And we may wonder: if we ask for what we need and are answered positively, what are we bound to do in return?

ברוך אתה שעשה
לי כל צרכי

*Barukh atah she'asah
li kol tzorki*

Blessed is the One who
provides for all my needs

Meditation

A Prayer for What I Need

We used to pray for wine, flour, oil.

We knew the deal:
We pleased You, and asked for the things
  we needed.
We expected You would come through.

I still need wine, flour, and oil,
But I do not ask for them.
(The market is just down the street.)

This does not mean You are off the hook.
As I see it, the deal stands:
My coming through,
My asking for what I cannot get alone.

These are the staples:
Love, health, work, protection.

And this is what I need now: _____.

I need to have the courage to call out to You
when I am in need.

I need You to be ready to hear me.

מן המצר קראתי יה, ענני במרחב יה.

*Min ha'meitzar karati Yah, anani
va'merchav Yah.*

I have called You from tight places,
You answered me with expansiveness.

Ritual

As you begin each day, either during the traditional
Amidah prayer or, perhaps, as you wait for your coffee,
set aside a fixed time to focus upon what you need that
you cannot achieve or acquire on your own. Then ask,
"Please, God, this is what I need now: _____ ."

Blessing

(After you have prayed for what you need)

ואני תפלתי לך ה' עת רצון,
אלקים ברב חסדך, ענני.

*Va'ani t'filati l'kha Adonai ayt ratzon, elohim b'rov
chasdekha, aneini.*

Hear my prayer now, and in Your compassionate ways,
please answer me.

ברוך אתה שעשה לי כל צרכי.

Barukh atah she'asah li kol tzorki.

Blessed is the One who provides for all my needs.

ברוך אתה שומע תפלה.

Barukh atah shomei'a t'filah.

Blessed is the One who hears my prayer.

Teaching

קרוב ה׳ לכל קראיו.

Karov Adonai l'khol kor'av.

God is close to all who call out.

(Ashrei)

According to R. Eliezer: If people pray only according to the exact text of the prayer and add nothing from their own minds, the prayer is not complete.

(Babylonian Talmud: Mishnah Brakhot 4:4)

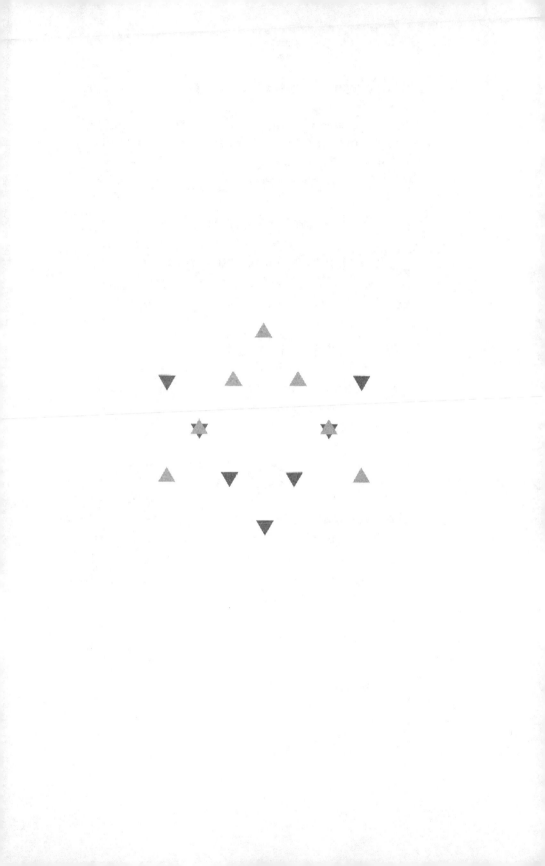

WASHING OUR HANDS

Hand washing separates us from what came before and prepares us for what's to come; it symbolizes our becoming conscious of what we do and who we are. The most familiar time for the ritual washing of hands is before meals, but there are other traditional times for special hand washing rituals. These include waking up in the morning and returning home from a cemetery.

עַל נְטִילַת יָדַיִם

Al netilat yadayim

Upon washing our hands

Meditation

Source of Blessing, may the washing of my hands cleanse me and direct my hands to doing deeds of righteousness.

Ritual

First, you may wish to remove any rings you are wearing. Then take a cup (preferably one with two handles) and fill it with water. With your left hand, hold the cup and pour three times over your right hand. Switch hands, repeat, lift up your hands, and then say the blessing.

Blessing

ברוך אתה ה׳ אלקינו מלך העולם
אשר קדשנו במצותיו וצונו על נטילת ידים.

*Barukh atah Adonai eloheinu melekh ha'olam, asher
kidshanu b'mitzvotav v'tzivanu al netilat yadayim.*

Blessed are You, Lord our God, whose *mitzvot* make our lives holy
and who gives us the *mitzvah* of washing our hands.

Teaching

Tradition specifies that for ritual washing, the water
be poured over the hands by human agency, not by
machine or faucet. The point is that awakening consciousness cannot be accomplished by mechanical
means. Usually you pour water on your own hands
(on the right hand first), but pouring can also be
done by someone else as a mark of love or friendship. It is also customary to be silent from the
moment of washing until the *challah* is broken and
eaten. The mind is concentrated, and consciousness
focuses on the bread and the meal to follow.

(*Irving [Yitz] Greenberg*, The Jewish Way)

EATING

The Rabbis of the Talmud once said different blessings for each kind of food. For delicacies, our rabbis said: "Blessed are You who created all kinds of delicacies for delight." For meats and eggs, they said: "Blessed are You who created life to give life." For bread: "Blessed are You who brings out bread from the earth." While some rabbis taught that only the proper "formula" could be recited over specific foods, others took a more pragmatic view, saying, "If you were to see a loaf of bread and say, 'What a fine loaf this is! Blessed is the Holy One who created it!' you would have fulfilled your obligation to bless" (Babylonian Talmud: *Brakhot* 6).

ברוך...שהכל
נהיה בדברו

*Barukh...she'ha'kol
n'hi'yeh b'dvaro*

Blessed are You...whose
word calls all things
into being

Meditation

When I sit down at the table, the Divine Presence stands behind me. When I say a blessing, the Divine Presence pushes forward to receive my words.

(Adapted from Zohar *IV:186b)*

Ritual

Before you are about to eat, pause just long enough to compose a blessing that recognizes the specific food that you are about to enjoy. As an example, our rabbis offer the blessing of a simple shepherd named Benjamin who made a sandwich and said, *"Brikh rachamana marai d'hai pita."* "Blessed be the Master of this bread."

(Babylonian Talmud: Brakhot *40b)*

Blessing

ברוך...שֶׁהַכֹּל נִהְיָה בִּדְבָרוֹ.

Barukh...she'ha'kol n'hi'yeh b'dvaro.

Blessed are You...whose word calls all things into being. (Offer the traditional blessing for specific foods, or add your own blessing to heighten your awareness of the source of your food.)

Teaching

Rabbi Yosi the Elder would not have his meal cooked until he prayed to God for sustenance. Then he waited a moment. Then he would say, "Now that the Sovereign has sent sustenance, let us prepare it."

(Zohar II:62b)

When you have eaten and you are satisfied, bless God for the good earth that has been entrusted to you.

(Deuteronomy 8:10)

Let us take time to bless that which gives us life— sweet as the fruit from Eden's tree, filling as Sarah's cakes, savory as Jacob's stew, plentiful as the manna in the wilderness, liberating as the crunchy matzah, fresh as the first harvest brought to the Temple, heavenly as the taste of the World to Come in the Shabbat *challah.*

(CLAL Faculty)

MAKING A LIST OF THINGS TO DO

Each morning my father consults his list of things to do, which is numbered clearly and prioritized on a long yellow pad. "Buy milk and shredded wheat" may be number one, or "Exercise bike at the JCC." Some days, other im-portant items appear, such as doctors' appointments, anniver-saries, birthdays, *shiva* calls, and preparations for holidays and vaca-tions. One thing is for sure: If it isn't on the list, it probably will not get done.

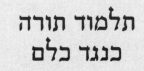

תלמוד תורה
כנגד כלם

Talmud Torah k'neged kulam

Study Torah, embracing all of life

Meditation

To do:

Teach children

Honor parents

Be where I am needed

Make study a priority

Welcome guests

Visit the sick

Help those who are
    starting out

Honor the dead

Pray with intensity

Make peace

And, most of all,

*Talmud Torah k'neged
    kulam.*

Study Torah:

The embrace of all life,

Leading to all that we
    value.

Ritual

Imagine beginning your day by writing out a sacred "to do" list, reminding you that opportunities to perform life's holiest tasks are not beyond you, not "in the heavens," but are right here in your daily encounters with family, friends, and strangers. What if you made your own "to do" list and noted the deeper dimensions and ethical implications presented by your own tasks—buying groceries, calling a lonely friend, repairing the car, paying bills, going for a checkup? Start out with the traditional sacred "to do" list. Then add the specific tasks you must perform this day, each a sacred opportunity.

Blessing

(When you have completed writing your list)

עֵץ חַיִּים הִיא לְמַחֲזִיקִים בָּהּ.

Eitz chaim hi la'machazikim bah.

Torah is a tree of life, embracing us as we embrace it.

Blessed are You who sanctifies us with *mitzvot* and commands us to make Torah concrete in our lives.

Teaching

Rabbi Yose said: "Apply yourself to study Torah, for it is not yours by inheritance, and let all your deeds be in the name of heaven."

(Pirkei Avot 2:17)

דור לדור ישבח מעשיך וגבורתיך יגידו.

Dor l'dor y'shabach ma'asekha,
u'gvurotekha yagidu.

Every generation will praise Your works to the next and will speak of Your powerful deeds.

(Ashrei)

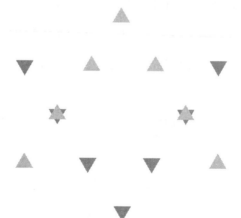

PREPARING A FAMILY RECIPE

You are about to cook a "traditional" family recipe—grandma's soups, your cousin's easy chocolate cake—or a "new traditional" recipe: your son's vegetable lasagna, your mother-in-law's low-fat latkes. These special foods connect you to people you love and who love you. They create a sense of home, no matter where you are, no matter how far away you've gone, no matter if those who taught you the recipes are no longer here.

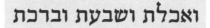

ואכלת ושבעת וברכת

V'akhalta, v'savata, u'veirakhta

And you shall eat, and you shall be satisfied, and you shall bless

Meditation

May my love and the love of all those who are connected to this recipe go into this food and bring joy.

Ritual

Before preparing your recipe: If your family recipe remains an oral tradition, now is the time to write it down. "Torah" must be written to assure its transmission from one generation to the next! Include on your recipe card a note about who gave it to you, the story behind the recipe, and any special memories and feelings it evokes. Make copies and share them with family members. Or consider gathering all your family's recipes and creating a family cookbook to celebrate, honor, or commemorate someone you love. Imagine a festive meal composed of many recipes!

Blessing

You sustain all life, providing us with foods that nourish life and
create nurturing memories.

ברוך אתה ה׳ הזן את הכל.

Barukh atah Adonai hazan et ha'kol.

Blessed is the One who gives us the food and the love
that sustains us.

Teaching

These are the offerings by fire that you are
to present to the Lord…and as a meal offering,
there shall be a tenth of an *ephah* of choice flour
with a quarter of a *hin* of beaten oil mixed in—the
regular burnt offering instituted at Mount Sinai—
an offering by fire of pleasing odor to the Lord.

(*Numbers 28:3–6*)

Although cooking is fragile because it lives in
human activity, it isn't easily destroyed. It is transmitted in every family like genes, and it has the
capacity for change and for passing on experience
from one generation to another.

(*Claudia Rodin,* The Book of Jewish Food)

GOING TO WORK

We pray that the work we do will be a source of blessing and success, so that we may support ourselves, our families, and our communities with the means necessary for shalom (peace) and *chaim* (life). May our work be more than just a means to an end; may we discover how to make our work and our workplace more soulful and dignified.

עבדו את ה' בשמחה

Ivdu et Adonai b'simchah

May your work be joyful, God's work

Meditation

May I and my work be valued. May others treat me respectfully, celebrating my successes and sustaining me when I need to try again. May my goals be high enough, my expectations be reasonable, and my work be in harmony with the rest of my life. May I treat the people I work with compassionately and value their contributions. May our patience always grow stronger.

יהי רצון שתשרה שכינה במעשי ידי.

Ye'hi ratzon shetishreh Shekhinah bema'asei yadai.

May it be Your will that the Divine Presence reside in all my work.

Ritual

Select a special object to bring to work that will remind you of the purpose of your work, your *melakha*. What could represent the principles you hold? Place the object where you can see it easily upon entering each morning. It will be like a mezuzah, an *ot*, a sign of who you are, what you believe, and the principles and values that guide you.

Blessing

(As you enter your workplace)

תן ברכה והצלחה בכל מעשי ידי לחיים ולשלום.

*Tein brakhah v'hatzlachah b'khol
ma'asei yadai l'chaim u'l'shalom.*

Bless me with success in all of my work, and let my work
increase life and peace.

Blessed are You who blesses us with prosperity.

Teaching

Six days you shall labor and do all your work.

(Deuteronomy 5:13)

It is beautiful when the study of Torah is combined with worldly work.

(Pirkei Avot 2:2)

Just as the Torah was given to us as a covenant, so was work.

(Avot d'Rabbi Natan *11:1*)

על שלושה דברים העולם עומד על התורה ועל העבודה ועל גמילות חסדים.

Al shlosha d'varim ha'olam omed: al ha'Torah, v'al ha'avodah, v'al gemilut chasadim.

The world is poised on three things: Torah, work, and the ways of kindness.

(Pirkei Avot *1:2*)

ORGANIZING YOUR ROOM, YOUR HOUSE, YOUR OFFICE, YOUR AFFAIRS, YOUR LIFE

When life is at its most chaotic, we often find ourselves restoring order by performing miniature, symbolic acts of repair. We may stand before the woolen singles bar that is a sock drawer, reuniting long-lost pairs, creating new matches.

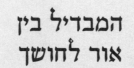

המבדיל בין
אור לחושך

Ha'mavdil bein or
l'choshekh

You separate the light
from the darkness

Meditation

I am grateful for all small gestures of ordering
that are possible to make; through them, I glimpse
possibilities of a more complex world where all is
ordered and all is one.

Ritual

Complete the activity of reordering (to the best of
your ability) and take a moment to witness your
accomplishment.

Blessing

(Upon restoring order)

ברוך המביא סדר לעולם.

Barukh ha'meivi seder la'olam.

Blessed is the One who brings order to the world, as You bless my
efforts to bring order.

Teaching

And the earth was without form and void, and
darkness was upon the face of the deep, and
a wind from God moved upon the face of the
waters. God said, "Let there be light," and there
was light.

(Genesis 1:2–3)

Blessed is the One who organizes the stars into
their heavenly constellations…who separates
between day and night.

(Ma'ariv)

לא עליך המלאכה לגמר.

Lo alekha ham'lakhah ligmor.

It is not necessary for you to complete the task.

(Pirkei Avot 2:21)

TRAVELING

The JCC Maccabi Games send young Jewish athletes to compete at various sites each summer. As the mom of a Maccabi athlete and wife of a Maccabi coach, I was curious to see what else was "Jewish" about these games, in addition to their providing a chance to meet other Jewish young people and Jewish host families and a chance to experience good sportsmanship as a Jewish value. I was touched to discover that all Maccabi athletes and coaches who were traveling to the games were given a wallet-sized *Tefilat Haderekh* (a prayer for travelers) card, an eloquent prayer and meditation for the travelers going from a familiar setting to a community they did not know. As I waved good-bye and good luck to our team, I felt they were being accompanied by a watchful eye.

ושמור צאתנו ובואנו

*U'shmor tzeiteinu
u'vo'einu*

Guard our comings and
our goings

Meditation

Why a prayer for traveling? We find security in familiar settings, among the people and in the places we know well. Therefore, traveling outside our community can make us feel a little uneasy. We ask God to "lead us forward in peace" because life itself is an endless journey in which we never really reach our destination. As Jews, we are always journeying toward peace, for ourselves, for our people, and for all of humankind.

(JCC Maccabi Games)

Ritual

As you prepare to depart on your journey, take a
moment to reflect on the wonder of being able to move

from one place to another, of being able to anticipate familiar and new experiences along the way. Now this part of the ritual is simple, but it must be done always: Buckle up!

Blessing

(After you have buckled up and are preparing to depart)

Ye'hi ratzon, may it be Your will, Lord my God, to lead me on the way of peace, and guide and direct my steps in peace, so that You will bring me happily to my destination, safe and sound. Save me from danger on the way. Give me good grace, kindness, and favor both in Your eyes and in the eyes of all whom I may meet. Hear this, my prayer, for You are a God who listens to the heart's supplication and communion. Blessed are You, Lord our God, who hears prayer.

(JCC Maccabi Games)

Teaching

What should one say on entering a city in the course of a journey? "May it be Your will, O Lord my God, to bring me into this city in peace." When about to leave, one should say, "May it be Your will, O Lord my God, to bring me out of this city in peace." When one is outside the city, one should say, "I give thanks to You, Lord my God, as You have brought me out of this city in peace, and as You brought me out in peace, so may You guide me in peace, support me in peace, and safeguard me from any danger along the way."

(Babylonian Talmud: Brakhot 60a)

KEEPING A SENSE OF HOME WHEN YOU ARE ON THE ROAD

How do we keep a sense of home when we are on the road? Being a people that has spent generations wandering, we have learned many ways to feel at home even when we must be away. The Talmud teaches that "in all the places that Samuel visited, his home was with him" (Babylonian Talmud: *Brakhot* 10b). How was it possible that wherever Samuel traveled, he always felt at home? Rashi explains that Samuel traveled with his tent and cooking utensils. We who find ourselves "away from home" and often feel disconnected may learn from this text a technique for bringing symbols of the warmth and comfort of our homes with us on our journeys.

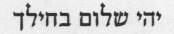

יהי שלום בחילך

Ye'hi shalom b'cheileikh

May there be peace within your walls

Meditation

מה טבו אהליך יעקב.

Mah tovu ohalekha Ya'akov!

How good are your dwellings, Jacob!

Ritual

When you are packing for a trip, bring small things that symbolically represent home to you. You might bring photographs, artwork, a book, a stone from your garden, a special food, a prayer book. If you will be away over the Sabbath, bring along your candles and a small bottle of wine for *kiddush*. If you will be away for a month or longer, you can bring a mezuzah and hang it (using a temporary fastener) on the door.

Blessing

(As you set up your home away from home)

ברוך שנתן שלום בחילך.

Barukh shenatan shalom b'cheileikh.

Blessed is the One who creates peace within these walls.

Teaching

May there be peace within your walls, serenity within your dwelling places.

(Psalms 122:7)

Through wisdom is a home built, and through understanding is it sustained. With knowledge the rooms will be filled with all things precious and pleasant.

(Proverbs 24:3–4)

SPENDING TIME WITH FAMILY

Driving five hours back home after spending Thanksgiving with family in Washington, I stare in wonder at all the other people who are also clearly returning from their own family gatherings. We all fulfilled this ritual scrupulously, many of us staying with our *mishpoche*, our relatives, for the rest of the weekend. Why? It's family.

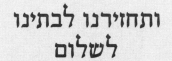

ותחזירנו לבתינו
לשלום

*Vatachzireinu l'veiteinu
l'shalom*

Allow us to discover peace
when we go home to family

Meditation

(Before arriving)

Let us spend these days together with a deepened
awareness of what the point of our being together
is; let us expand the possibilities of our relating to
each other beyond the various family stereotypes
and patterns we tend to replay. Let us be clever and
sparkling for each other, or still and receptive; let us
lean into our familiarity so that we can challenge,
take risks, support each other in going out on new
limbs. When it is time to pack up the car again and
return to our separate homes, let us be changed, let
us have grown, let us feel supported.

Ritual

Create a T-shirt or hat with some kind of "tribal" emblem that signifies what it means to be a member of your family, and bring one for everyone to wear.

Blessing

וּפְרוֹשׁ עָלֵינוּ סֻכַּת שְׁלוֹמֶךָ,
וְתַקְּנֵנוּ בְּעֵצָה טוֹבָה מִלְּפָנֶיךָ.

Ufros aleinu sukkat shlomekha v'takneinu b'aytzah tovah mil'fanekha.

You have given us a home, a shelter of peace, and guided us to return home with wisdom.

בָּרוּךְ אַתָּה עוֹשֶׂה הַשָּׁלוֹם.

Barukh atah oseh ha'shalom.

Blessed are You who creates peace.

יְהִי רָצוֹן שֶׁתַּחֲזִירֵנוּ לְמִשְׁפַּחְתֵּינוּ לְשָׁלוֹם.

Ye'hi ratzon shetachzireinu l'mishpachteinu l'shalom.

Allow us to discover peace and wholeness when we go home to family.

Teaching

"And you must tell my father everything about my high station in Egypt and all that you have seen; and bring my father here with all speed." With that, he (Joseph) embraced his brother Benjamin around the neck and wept, and Benjamin wept on his neck. He kissed all his brothers and wept upon them; only then were his brothers able to talk to him. The news reached Pharaoh's palace: "Joseph's brothers have come."

(Genesis 45:13–16)

Lo, I will send the prophet Elijah to you before the coming of the awesome, fearful day of the Lord. He shall reconcile parents with children and children with their parents.

(Malachi 3:23–24)

I will be your partner forever.

(Midrash Pesikta Rabbati)

HAVING GUESTS OF DIFFERENT FAITHS AT OUR TABLE

Guests of different faiths often bring questions to our table. "What is this food called?" "What does that blessing mean?" "Do you do this every night?" In answering their questions, we engage in a process of dialogue and discovery. From tablecloths to recipes to the words we speak, outsiders often help us to appreciate the things that we overlook. Inviting them to our table and sharing a meal is truly a blessing, not just of fellowship but of new insight.

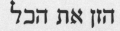

הזן את הכל

Hazan et ha'kol

You sustain all life

Meditation

May it be Your will that just as we have sat down and eaten together at this table in peace, so should all people be able to sit down and eat together in peace. Sustain us through Your goodness, mercy, love, and compassion to complete Your holy work of perfecting the world.

Ritual

The ritual is simple. As you take your seats around the table, take a moment to become more aware of those with whom you are about to share this meal. Offer words of welcome.

Blessing

הנה מה טוב ומה נעים שבת אחים גם יחד.

Hinei mah tov u'mah na'im shevet achim gam yachad.

How good it is to sit together as brothers and sisters.

ברוך אתה ה' אלקינו מלך העולם
המוציא לחם מן הארץ.

Barukh atah Adonai eloheinu melekh ha'olam, ha'motzi lechem min ha'aretz.

Blessed are You, our God, who sustains us with bread
from the earth.

Teaching

For the Lord Your God…loves the stranger, providing the stranger with food and clothing. And you
too shall love the strangers, for you were strangers
in the land of Egypt.

(Deuteronomy 10:17–19)

And the foreigners who join themselves to the Lord
and hold fast my covenant…these I will bring to
my holy mountain, and make them joyful in my
house of prayer; their burnt offerings and their sacrifices will be accepted on my altar; for my house
shall be called a house of prayer for all peoples.

(Isaiah 56:6–7)

BRINGING HOME A NEW PET

Your heart has been claimed. The animal you see at a shelter, at a breeder's, in a cozy box huddled with tiny siblings on your friend's porch—says with its persuasive eyes, "Take me home! Yes, you!" Providing a home for an animal is a *mitzvah*, a great kindness for one of God's creatures. (Children whose parents are big on Jewish values take note: Your parents may find this line of argument irresistible even if all others fail. So with all the conviction you can muster, say, "But Mom, Dad, it's a *mitzvah!*")

מרחם על הבריות

Meracheim al ha'briyot

You embrace all creatures

Meditation

You have created this wonderful animal, and we are blessed to care for Your creation. May we be blessed by the joy given to one creature in the company of another.

Ritual

Before you bring home your new pet, find the right space for it to live. Set aside a water bowl, a food dish, a sleeping place, and, for a cat, a litter box. Gently introduce your new pet to your home and to the place of its own. You'll discover that petting, and all your caring rituals, are a comfort for you and for your pet.

When brainstorming to find just the right name for your new pet, consider a Hebrew name that evokes a trait your pet seems to embody, for example: Sweetness (*Motek*), Beauty (*Yofi*), Simplicity (*Tam*), Happiness (*Simcha*), Strength (*Ko'ach*), Life (*Chaim*), Noisiness (*Ra'ash*).

Blessing

(As you bring your new pet into your home for the first time)

ברוך מרחם על הבריות.

Barukh meracheim al ha'briyot.

Blessed is the One who embraces all creatures.

Teaching

God formed every living thing...and brought each to the human to see what he would call it, and whatever the human called it, that became its name.

(Genesis 2:19)

How many things You have made, O God; You have made them wisely; the earth is filled with Your creations.

(Psalms 104:24)

A man may eat nothing until he has fed his animals.

(Babylonian Talmud: Brakhot 40a)

It is a good sign *(siman tov)* when one's animal eats and is satisfied, and so it says, "Righteous persons know the souls of their animals."

(Yalkut Shimeoni, *commentary on Deuteronomy 11:15*)

GARDENING

In the backyard, by the wall, we planted a garden. With each bulb, seed, and plant that we tucked into the earth, we wondered—which will flourish and which will fail to thrive?

And when the first strawberry grew, and we plucked it, washed it, and tasted it right there in the sun, we connected ourselves to the Source of Creation in one bite.

נודה לך על שהנחלת לאבותינו ארץ חמדה טובה ורחבה

Nodeh l'kha al she'hinchalta la'avoteinu eretz chemdah tovah ur'chavah

We thank You for the pleasing, good, and spacious land that You gave our ancestors

Meditation

I will respond to the sky, and it shall respond to the earth; and the earth shall respond with new grain and wine and oil.

(Hosea 2:23–24)

I have planted my garden with hope and trust. Let me be awake to the wonder of this garden. As I tend to this garden, let me tend to my own capacity to sustain life.

Ritual

At each phase of the planting process, pause to consider what you can accomplish alone and what you cannot accomplish alone.

Blessing

(Upon planting)

גן רוח שימנו בטל, טל בו תברך מזון. ברוך אתה מוריד הטל.

Gan raveh simeinu b'tal, tal bo t'varcich mazon.
Barukh atah morid ha'tal.

Blessed are You who sustains us with what we need: water, light, and growth.

(Upon harvesting and upon tasting fruits for the first time in the season)

ברוך אתה ה׳ אלקינו מלך העולם שהחינו וקימנו והגיענו לזמן הזה.

Barukh atah Adonai eloheinu melekh ha'olam
shehecheyanu v'kiy'manu v'higi'anu lazman hazeh.

Blessed are You who has kept us in life, sustained us, and enabled us to reach this season.

Teaching

The Lord God planted a garden in Eden, in the east, and placed there the human whom God had formed. And from the ground the Lord God caused to grow every tree that was pleasing to the sight and good for food, with the tree of life in the middle of the garden, and the tree of knowledge of good and bad.

(Genesis 2:8–9)

Isaac set to work and planted because he knew that true blessings only come when you labor with your hands.

(Tosefta Brakhot *6:13*)

שתולים בבית ה׳ בחצרות אלקינו יפריחו.

Shetulim b'vayt Adonai b'chatzrot eloheinu yafrichu.

(Psalms 92:14)

How do we know that God also gardens? From the Psalms, for it says that "tiny plants in God's house, in God's backyard, will flourish."

(CLAL Faculty)

PARENTS AND CHILDREN

HOPING TO HAVE A CHILD

Our ancestor Rachel cried out, "Give me children, or I shall die." So many thousands of male and female "Rachels" are among us who also pray and hope for a child with the very same passion and intensity. In a community that so loves children, those who experience difficulty conceiving or adopting are all the more passionate and intense in their prayers.

כי בנו בחרת,
ואותנו קדשת

*Ki vanu vacharta,
v'otanu kidashta*

You have chosen us and
have given us sacred
purposes in life

Meditation

May it be Your will to choose us for sacred purposes in life.

Ritual

For a special *aliyah* on *Shabbat Vayeitzei* when we read about Rachel who yearned for a child (Genesis 30:1), we call up to the Torah all those who are thinking about one day having children or grandchildren, all those who are trying to have children, and all those who are hoping to be successful in adoption. As you hear the Torah chanted, let the words of Rachel's yearning strengthen you, and may your hopes be realized. (The first day of Rosh Hashanah, when we chant the Haftarah in which Hannah prays for a child, is another time to enact this ritual.)

NOTE: If group *aliyot* are not the custom of your community, you may choose to mark *Shabbat Vayeitzei* by intensifying your concentration as the passages of Rachel's yearning for a child are chanted.

Blessing

(The person who is called to the Torah)

ברכו את ה׳ המברך.

Barkhu et Adonai ha'm'vorakh.

Blessed are You, Source of Blessing.

(The congregation responds)

ברוך ה׳ המברך לעולם ועד.

Barukh Adonai ha'm'vorakh l'olam va'ed.

Blessed are You, Source of Blessing, forever.

ברוך אתה ה׳ אלקינו מלך העולם,
אשר בחר בנו מכל העמים, ונתן לנו את תורתו.
ברוך אתה ה׳ נותן התורה.

*Barukh atah Adonai eloheinu melekh ha'olam, asher
bachar banu mi'kol ha'amim v'natan lanu et Torato.
Barukh atah Adonai notein ha'Torah.*

Blessed are You, Lord our God, Sovereign of the Universe, who
has chosen us from among all peoples by giving us Your Torah.
Praised are You, Lord, who gives the Torah.

Teaching

But Abram said, "God, what can You give me, seeing that I shall die childless?" God took him outside and said, "Look toward heaven and count the stars...so shall your offspring be."

(Genesis 15:2,5)

The Lord took note of Sarah....Sarah conceived...and said, "God has brought me laughter."

(Genesis 21:1,2,6)

Now God remembered Rachel; God heeded her and opened her womb.

(Genesis 30:22)

וראה בנים לבניך. שלום על ישראל.

Ur'ei vanim l'vanekha.
Shalom al Yisrael.

May you live to see your children's children.

Peace be upon Israel.

(Psalms 128:6)

CELEBRATING PREGNANCY

A father-to-be tells this story: You have to wait five minutes for the results to appear on the pregnancy testing device. My wife handed me the device and jumped under the blankets waiting for the results. It was during Sukkot, so naturally I prayed. I held up the pregnancy test device as a *lulav* before me. I gently shook it in the six directions, praying for all those who seek fertility, and praying for us. Then I peeked. Yes!! I crawled under the covers and whispered the good news.

בשעה טובה
ומוצלחת

*Besha'ah tovah
u'mutzlachat*

May all go as it should

Meditation

Oh God, I pray that this child will be healthy,
I pray that I will be a good parent,
I pray that I will be able to provide for this child,
Oh God, let this baby be born!

Ritual

(For expecting parents and those who have heard
their good news)

Prepare a meal for the parent-to-be, selecting from this rabbinic menu: "One who eats eggs will have children with big eyes. One who eats fish will have graceful children. One who eats parsley will have beautiful children. One who eats coriander will have hearty children. One who eats *etrog* will have fragrant children. The daughter of King Shapur, whose mother had eaten *etrog* [while she was pregnant] with her, used to be presented before her father as his principal perfume.

(Babylonian Talmud: Ketubot 61a)

Let your symbolic meal inspire discussion of the values you are hoping to transmit to the soon-to-be child.

Blessing

ברוך אתה הטוב והמטיב.

Barukh atah ha'tov v'hameitiv.

Blessed are You whom we thank for this good news.

בשעה טובה ומוצלחת.

Besha'ah tovah u'mutzlachat.

May all go as it should.

Teaching

I entreat You, Lord, God of Israel, accept my prayer, just as You accepted the prayer of our mother [Hannah] when she prayed for her son [Samuel]. And may her merit assist me, so that I…may bear to full term this child that I now carry in my womb…and that a healthy child may emerge. May my child be a…Jew, serving You with heart and soul, loving Torah and being in awe of heaven, according to Your holy will. May my child be a beautiful seedling in the Jewish vineyard for the glory of [Israel]. Amen.

(Tkhine: The Merit of Our Mothers,
Tracy Guren Klirs, ed.)

Within the first three days, pray that the seed remain viable…. From the fortieth day to three months, pray that it flourish. From three months to six months, pray that it reach full term. From six months to nine months, pray for safe delivery.

(Adapted from Babylonian Talmud: Brakhot *60a)*

A mother-to-be tells this story: When the doctor called to say that I was pregnant, we wanted to keep the news a secret for a while. But the moment our landlords, an elderly German-Jewish couple, asked me what was new, I told them. They hugged me and hugged each other, saying, "There is *mazel* in our bed."

WELCOMING A NEW CHILD

The arrival of a child is a most wondrous miracle. When your child is born or when you welcome your grandchild, you may well be at a loss for words, so awesome is the event you have just experienced! A special ceremony, to be held on your child's first Shabbat at home, celebrates the light a new child brings to life.

אוֹר חָדָשׁ עַל
צִיּוֹן תָּאִיר

Or chadash al tzion ta'ir

A new light is lit

Meditation

Just as my child has arrived safely into the world and into my life, may my child be blessed with abundant love, guidance, and protection.

Enable me to be fully present for this new and wondrous life.

Help me to be a wise and loving parent. Help me to be patient and kind, to be a teacher and worthy model. And when I need support, may the community provide a home and haven for this child through the years.

Ritual

On the first Shabbat of your child's life, begin lighting an additional Shabbat candle to represent this new light that fills your heart and your home.

Blessing

(As you light the Shabbat candles)

ברוך אתה ה׳ אלקינו מלך העולם
אשר קדשנו במצותיו וצונו להדליק נר של שבת.

*Barukh atah Adonai eloheinu melekh ha'olam asher
kidshanu b'mitzvotav v'tzivanu l'hadlik ner
shel shabbat.*

Blessed are You who makes us holy with *mitzvot* and commands
us to light the Shabbat candles.

(Offer a personal blessing for your child)

May my child be blessed with:

_____ .

(As you light your child's candle the first time)

ברוך אתה ה׳ אלקינו מלך העולם
שהחינו וקימנו והגיענו לזמן הזה.

*Barukh atah Adonai eloheinu melekh ha'olam
shehecheyanu v'kiy'manu v'higi'anu lazman hazeh.*

Blessed are You who has kept us in life, sustained us, and enabled
us to reach this season.

Teaching

We are partners in the creation of a person: The
Holy One and us.

(Adapted from Babylonian Talmud: Kiddushin 30b)

Grant that I be worthy of giving life to knowing,
wise, and distinguished children...may they light
up the world through their learning and kindness.

(Out of the Depths I Call You, *Rabbi Nina
Beth Cardin, ed.*)

As you light your candles, so may your child's
eyes be illuminated by Torah, by the wisdom of
the world, by nature, and by people.

(CLAL Faculty)

NURSING

Just as God nurtures us, sustaining us with food and all that we need, we who nurse or feed our babies sustain them. The experience of nursing a child brings the text of *Birkat Hamazon* (Grace after Meals) to mind. We share this *kavanah* (meditation) by Elisheva S. Urbas of New York City, published originally in *Sh'ma*.

ברוך אתה ה׳
הזן את הכל

*Barukh atah Adonai
hazan et ha'kol*

Blessed are You who
provides food for all

Meditation

God of our mothers, Sarah, Rebecca, Rachel, and Leah, You remembered me when I longed for this child and when I was in the pain of labor, and You have brought me, rejoicing, to hold this infant in my arms. Now I turn to You again, hoping to feed this child as You feed all living creatures, out of Your boundless lovingkindness.

Ritual

Each time you nurse or feed your child, whisper this blessing for food so that it will become a quiet, deep memory. And do not forget to nourish and care for yourself!

Blessing

(As you nurse or feed your child)

ברוך אתה ה׳ הזן את הכל.

Barukh atah Adonai hazan et ha'kol.

Blessed are You who provides food for all.

(Grace after Meals)

Teaching

And who would have believed, and told Abraham, that Sarah would nurse her children?

(Genesis 21:7)

That you may nurse and be satisfied with the breasts of comfort, may the milk delight you with its abundant glory.

(Isaiah 66:11)

And the people will nurse on the abundance of the seas and the treasures hidden in the sands.

(Deuteronomy 33:19)

GUIDING OUR GROWING CHILDREN TOWARD INDEPENDENCE

A message to my children: Your life will be filled with challenges, for you and for me. My hope for you, as you grow in independence and make your own decisions, is that we will always be open to one another; that after all arguments, there will be reconciliation and a recommitment to the love that holds us together.

ברוך שפטרני
מעונשו של זה

*Barukh she'petarani
mei'onsho shel zeh*

Blessed are You who prepares me to release my child at the right times

Meditation

May you flourish as you become who you are meant to be.

Ritual

As your children step out on their own for the first time—walking, sleeping in a bed, going to school, riding a bike, dating, traveling on their own, going to camp, graduating, going to work, marrying, having their own children—pause to acknowledge how much courage they have.

Blessing

(As you are privileged to witness your child's independence)

ברוך שפטרני מעונשו של זה.

Barukh she'petarani mei'onsho shel zeh.

Blessed are You who prepares me to release my child
at the right times.

Teaching

Why did God decide to create humans? Out of
loneliness? Curiosity? A need to be loved? A need
for creative, thinking, feeling partners? Whatever
the reason, God had some fine hopes and pinned
them all on the Big Plan: Give us freedom and
make us images of God. God then lived through
the generations of humans who were disappoint-
ing, who fell short, who denied or undermined the
Plan, or who were just plain evil—along with folks
who were loving and cared and stood up to injus-
tice and fought suffering. The miracle of life, the
real miracle, is that God stuck with us for so long,
instead of throwing in the towel and just giving up
the whole painful, frustrating exercise. Talk about
patience! Apparently God has simply never given
up the hope, planted before Eden, that with our
freedom and our independence we will eventually
perfect the world.

(CLAL Faculty)

PREPARING FOR YOUR BAR OR BAT MITZVAH

The months before a bar/bat mitzvah can be frenetic for both parents and teenagers. It may help to keep this thought in the back of your minds: you are all about to set out on a spiritual journey, a search for nothing less than the ultimate source of meaning in your lives.

נעשה ונשמע

Na'aseh v'nishma

First we do things, later we understand

Meditation

(For the bar or bat mitzvah)

יהי רצון מלפניד:

Ye'hi ratzon mil'fanekha:

May it be Your will: that as I study and review Torah, turning it and turning it and making it my own, I will find everything in it.

Ritual

To keep perspective during the months before a bar or bat mitzvah, set a moment aside on the day your preparations officially begin: this might be when you receive a date for the bar or bat mitzvah, or on the day tutoring or classes begin. On index cards, parents and their children can each write down one sentence that will remind them of one spiritual goal they might attain during this year of intense study and preparation. Post the index cards on the refrigerator, and keep on track by consulting the cards often.

Blessing

(For parents and children, after posting the index cards)

ברוך אתה ה' אלקינו מלך העולם
אשר קדשנו במצותיו וצונו לעסוק בדברי תורה.

Barukh atah Adonai eloheinu melekh ha'olam asher kidshanu b'mitzvotav v'tzivanu la'asok b'divrei Torah.

We praise You for the *mitzvot*, which make our lives holy, and for the *mitzvah* of studying the words of Torah.

May the words of Torah be sweet in our mouths and in the mouths of all Your people so that we, our children, and all the children of Israel may come to love You and study Torah for all the right reasons.

Teaching

ה' אלקיכם אמת.

Adonai eloheichem emet.

I, the Lord, am your God.

(Numbers 15:41)

Yehudah ben Tema taught: at thirteen, you gain responsibility for the *mitzvot*.

(Pirkei Avot 5:24)

Ben Hay-Hay taught: the reward is proportionate to the effort.

(Pirkei Avot 5:26)

The sages said, "One should always engage in the study of Torah, even if not for its own sake, for one who begins thus will end by studying for its own sake."

(Adapted from Maimonides, Laws of Torah Study *3:5)*

SENDING A CHILD TO COLLEGE

First they left home for overnights, then summer camp. But this time, as they leave for college, it feels so different. College means a new world, a new life, and an independence that makes us both proud and anxious. There's no deny-ing it, we realize, as we help pack up duffels and load up the car with the lamp, the computer, the CD player, the stuffed animals—they are ready to take this big step. We bless them, and in doing so we realize that we are ready, too.

דעה בינה והשכל

Dayah, binah, v'haskeil

Knowledge, understanding, and wisdom

Meditation

Setting off on this journey, may all your comings and goings be blessed.

Ritual

(Before leaving home)

Invite all those closest to the college-bound student (family, friends, teachers) to circle him or her as each gives a personal blessing (best to write the blessing out in advance, so it can be well thought out and permanent) and a photograph or small article that has special meaning. Place all the blessings in a special box that can be brought to school.

(After unpacking and setting up the new college residence)

Celebrate this big moment—moving into a college room—by presenting your child with a special Jewish ritual object for school. It could be a mezuzah, a menorah, Sabbath candles, a *tzedakah* box, a picture of the whole family, packages of instant chicken soup.

Blessing

(After receiving the circle of blessings, all recite)

> May God bless you and keep you.
> May God look kindly upon you.
> May God embrace you tenderly,
> and give you peace.

Teaching

> Go forth from your land and from your people and from your parents' home to a place that I will show you.
>
> *(Genesis 12:1)*

> You graciously give us the power to learn and grow in wisdom. Grant us knowledge, understanding, and wisdom.
>
> *(Adapted from the* Amidah)

Ilana has two doors in her college dorm room, and both have a mezuzah on them. One is made out of "Sculpy," a claylike material, and the other is silver. Ilana feels that a mezuzah is a sign to her of "comfort and community." School is not a permanent place to live, but Ilana always has a reminder of her personal home and of her home in a greater community because of the mezuzah.

(Jessica Wolpe)

BLESSING ONE'S PARENTS

As a child, my parents could do no wrong. As an adolescent, my parents could do no right. Now, as a parent myself, I finally understand why a pri- mary metaphor for the complicated and changing relationship between God and humans is that of parent and child.

הרחמן הוא יברך
את אבי מורי,
ואת אמי מורתי

Harachaman hu y'varekh et avi mori v'et imi morati.

Merciful One, bless my father, my teacher; and my mother, my teacher.

Meditation

Thank you for the traits you have modeled,
for showing me that love can overcome obstacles,
for sharing celebration and pain,
for teaching me about fragility and strength.

Ritual

If you are a child, call your parents with a blessing as your message. If you are a parent, experience accepting the blessings your children give you, however they are expressed.

Blessing

הרחמן הוא יברך את אבי מורי ואת אמי מורתי.

Harachaman hu y'varekh et avi mori v'et imi morati.

Merciful One,
May You bless my father, my teacher; and my mother, my teacher;
who have made a home for me.

May we all be blessed as You blessed my grandparents and
great-grandparents: in every possible way.

That is how we wished to be blessed,
everyone together, a complete blessing. Amen.

Teaching

The hearts of the parents will be turned toward the
children, and the hearts of the children will be
turned toward the parents.

(Malachi 3:24)

My child, heed the discipline of your father, and do
not forget the Torah of your mother, for they are a
graceful wreath on your head, a necklace around
your throat.

(Proverbs 1:8–9)

Blessed are You our God, God of our Mothers and
Fathers: God of Abraham, God of Isaac, God of
Jacob, God of Sarah, God of Rebecca, God of
Rachel, and God of Leah, who recalls the blessing
of our parents.

(Adapted from the Amidah*)*

RELATIONSHIPS

FALLING IN LOVE

Jacob went to the well,
I read,
But its mouth was blocked by a stone,
So he spoke with
the other
shepherds.
In the distance,
Rachel, with her
father's flock,
approached.
She saw him,
and he her.
Before he spoke,
He rolled away the
stone.

She approached him and they
kissed.
Then he wept.

ישקני מנשיקות פיהו,
כי טובים דודיך מיין

*Yishakeini m'nishikot
pihu, ki tovim dodekha
mi'yayin*

Kiss me with the kisses of
your mouth, for your love
is better than wine

But it is the
stone that I
remember,
Rolling away
the stone that
I thought
would be there
forever,
Opening up to the
deep waters.

Meditation

May we fully celebrate this love, allowing it to blossom
and keeping open to its possibilities. God of our ancestors, may You be present in our lives and our love.

Ritual

As you celebrate an anniversary of an important relationship, recall "the well" at which you first met, and
tell each other the story of your falling in love. Toast
l'chaim, rejoicing in your lives and your love. Describe
the new "wells" that deepen your love, the different
ways you nourish and strengthen each other. Bless
each other, and receive the blessing of those who
join in your celebration.

Blessing

(Bless each other)

בָּרוּךְ שֶׁבָּרָא אַהֲבָה וְאַחֲוָה וְשָׁלוֹם וְרֵעוּת.

Barukh shebara ahavah v'achavah v'shalom v'rei'ut.

Blessed is the One who creates love, harmony, peace,
and companionship.

(Bless those whose love for each other you celebrate)

Grant perfect joy to these loving companions.

בָּרוּךְ הַמְשַׂמֵחַ רֵעִים הָאֲהוּבִים.

Barukh ha'mesame'ach rei'im ha'ahuvim.

Blessed is the One who creates and sustains the joy of your love.

Teaching

And Rebecca lifted up her eyes when she saw Isaac.

(Genesis 24:64)

When Jacob saw Rachel...he kissed Rachel and
lifted up his voice and wept.

(Genesis 29:10–11)

My dove, in the hidden places of the rock, in the
secret places of the cliff, let me see your face, let me
hear your voice, for your voice is sweet and your
presence is lovely.

(Song of Songs 2:14)

CELEBRATING THE DIFFERENCE YOU'VE MADE IN EACH OTHER'S LIVES

At times, we are messengers for each other. Like angels, who go about the task of infusing the world with sacred meaning, each one of us has tried, in some way, to make each relationship and encounter meaningful. We know that without each other, without our synergy, we'd never have accomplished all that we did. Let us celebrate all the ways that we nurture and support one another.

ברוך אתה שמקיים
רצונך על ידינו

Barukh atah shemekayeim ritzonkha al yadeinu

Blessed are You, Eternal God, who fulfills Your vision through our hands

Meditation

We have been, for each other, messengers, catalysts, conduits of energy. We have created connections between heaven and earth. By making a difference in each other's lives, we have brought each other a step closer to being more complete. Whether we meant to play this role or it just seemed to happen, we have been, for each other, angels: messengers of divine purpose in the world. Only through each of our unique contributions could we complete our works together.

Ritual

When you reach the conclusion of a project, a class, a board meeting or a retreat, and when the time to part has come for people who have been together, acknowledge the many ways—known and unknown—that you have touched each other's lives. Share words that celebrate the contribution others have made to your life. Offer thanks for the specific gifts you have received, beginning: "I thank you for…."

Blessing

(When all the words of thanks have been shared)

ברוך אתה ה' שולח מלאכים.

Barukh atah Adonai sholei'ach malakhim.

Blessed are You, Eternal God, who dispatches angels.

צאתכם לשלום, מלאכי השלום, מלאכי עליון.

Tzeitkhem l'shalom, malakhei hashalom, malakhei elyon.

May we depart in peace, messengers of peace, messengers of the most High.

Teaching

And all the angels supported the weight of the heavenly work by joining one to another.

(V'khulam M'kablim)

When the Torah students in Pumbedita would part from each other, they would say:

מחיה חיים יתן לך חיים ארוכים וטובים ומתוקנין.

M'chayeh chaim yiten l'kha chaim arukim v'tovim um'tukanin.

May God, who gives life, give you a life that is long, good, and harmonious.

(Babylonian Talmud: Yoma 71a)

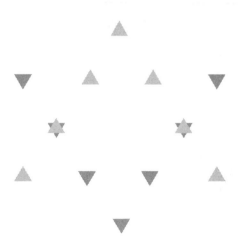

ENDING A RELATIONSHIP

I can tell our relationship is ending. As the full force of our breaking up hits me, I pray: "Please, God, don't let this end. Don't take my love away from me." I say this aloud for half an hour, until my prayer begins to change. My face still stinging with tears, I pray: "Please God, show me the way."

הרופא לשבורי לב ומחבש לעצבותם

Ha'rofei l'shvirei lev u'm'chabesh l'atzvotam

God heals the broken-hearted and binds up their sorrows

Meditation

May You who heals broken hearts lead me to discover the wholeness of my heart.

ה' ברצונך העמדתה להררי עז הסתרת פניך הייתי נבהל.

Adonai birtzonkha he'emadeta l'hariri oz, histarta fanekha ha'yiti nivhal.

When You are pleased, You make me as steady as a mountain. When You hide Your face, I am terrified.

(Psalms 30:8)

Ritual

To revive a broken heart: Gather your best friends. Get ready by washing your hair, getting dressed up. Pass out a broom, a Dustbuster, and sweep out your house. Choose some photos of you and your "ex" and tell their stories. When you're through, do not burn or throw the photos away! Place them in a sealed envelope, taking this part of your life out of the "active file."

Blessing

(When you gather friends for a "heart-mending")

Blessed are You, Creator of love and hope, Source of all the living, give me wisdom and understanding. Guide me as I step away from the one with whom I can no longer share my life. Guide me as I move forward and give me the strength to trust and love again.

ובטובו מחדש בכל יום תמיד מעשה בראשית.

Uv'tuvo m'chadesh b'khol yom tamid ma'asei v'reishit.

Creation renews itself every day, in goodness.

ברוך אתה מחיה כל חי.

Barukh atah mechayeh kol chai.

Blessed is the One who restores our spirits.

Teaching

חזק, חזק, ונתחזק.

Chazak, chazak, v'nitchazeik.

Strengthen us, strengthen us, and we shall become strong.

(Torah service)

צופה ויודע סתרינו מביט לסוף דבר בקדמתו.

Tzofeh v'yodea s'tareinu mabit l'sof davar b'kadmato.

You know all our secret thoughts, intuiting the end of things at their birth.

(Yigdal)

סומך ה׳ לכל הנופלים, וזוקף לכל הכפופים.

Somekh Adonai l'khol ha'noflim v'zokeif l'khol hak'fufim.

God supports all who stumble, raising all who are bowed down.

(Ashrei)

Nothing is as whole as a broken heart.

(Rabbi Nachman of Bratzlav)

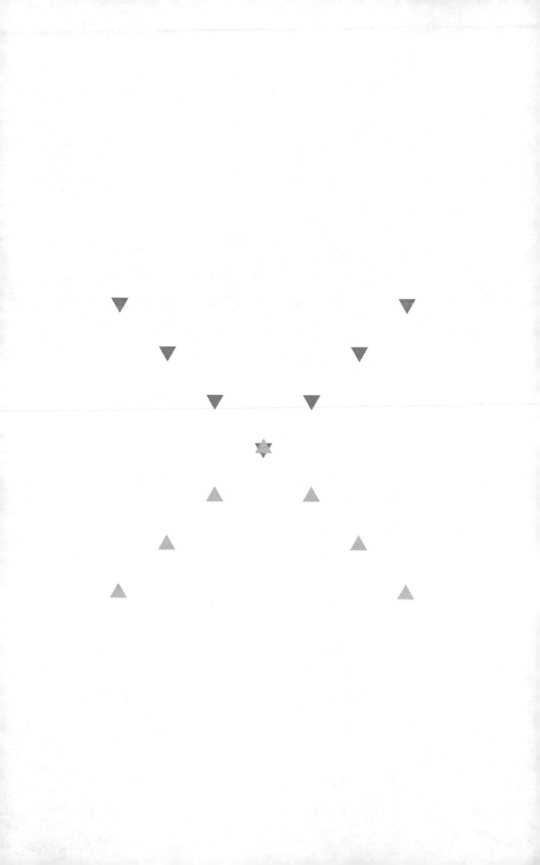

HEALING RELATIONSHIPS

Every relationship endures conflicts and disappointments that strain or wound. Being images of God, we can learn about mending a strained relationship from God's reconciliation with humanity after the flood. God placed a rainbow in the clouds to remind us that the covenant, the eternal relationship between God and humanity, is strong enough to survive conflict. To mend after human conflicts, we need to see the "rainbows" between us and affirm: we can get past this.

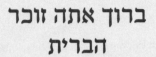

ברוך אתה זוכר
הברית

*Barukh atah zokheir
ha'brit*

Blessed are You who
remembers relationships

Meditation

This is the sign of the covenant that I set between Me and you…when the rainbow is in the clouds, I will look at it and remember our covenant.

(Genesis 9:15,16)

The rainbow is a sign of peace, wholeness, and permanence; it signals accepting limits for the sake of healing a broken world.

(Irving [Yitz] Greenberg, The Jewish Way)

הנה מה טוב ומה נעים שבת אחים גם יחד.

*Hinei mah tov u'mah na'im shevet achim
gam yachad.*

It's good to be together in relationship again.

Ritual

When a conflict has severely strained or wounded a relationship, and you succeed in coming together, even to sit in the same room or eat bread at the same table, *dayenu!* It is sufficient and admirable. This is particularly true for families that have been stressed by conflict: if you find yourselves together at a wedding, a seder, a birth, a funeral, *dayenu!* Just coming together once again is sufficient and admirable. Beyond this, be attentive to the "rainbows" between you, signs of enduring commitment: the same things that make you laugh, the concerns you share, your memories. If the moment is right, speak of the "rainbows" you share or create new ones.

Blessing

(When you commit yourself to the possibility of mending your relationship)

ברוך אתה זוכר הברית.

Barukh atah zokheir ha'brit.

Blessed are You who remembers that relationships are for keeps.

Help us to see the rainbows between us and to trust the power of our connection.

Teaching

Jacob and Esau had become bitter enemies, according to midrash. Childhood rivalries led to threats, fear, and years of estrangement. After decades of separation, however, they came together. "Esau ran to greet Jacob. He embraced him and, falling on his neck, he kissed him. And they wept...and Jacob said..., 'I have seen your face, as one sees the face of God.'"

(Genesis 33:4,10)

When two Babylonian sages disagree with each other about the law, there is no untruth there. Each justifies his opinion. One gives a reason to permit, the other a reason to forbid. One compares the case before him to one precedent, the other compares it to a different precedent. It is possible to say, "Both speak the word of the living God." At times, one reason is valid; at other times, the other reason is. Reasons change, even small alterations in the situation.

(Rashi, Babylonian Talmud: Ketubot 57a)

RECEIVING GUESTS

We want everything to be just right for our guests: the house in order, the table sparkling, the food lavish. It is an enchanting moment when the doorbell rings and the guests have arrived! When we perform the *mitzvah* of *hakhnasat orchim*, receiving guests, the pleasure is all ours.

ברוכים הבאים
בשם ה׳

*Brukhim ha'ba'im
b'sheim Adonai*

Blessed are you who have
come in God's name

Meditation

יהי רצון מלפניך שתשרה שכינתך בינינו.

*Ye'hi ratzon mil'fanekha she'tishreh
shechinat'kha beineinu.*

May it be Your will for Your presence to reside among us.

Ritual

When your guests arrive, there are many things you tend to say: "Welcome. How was your trip? Would you like a drink?" As you offer your greetings in your customary manner, recall how our contemporary greetings evoke the greetings of our ancestors: "God bless you!" "God be with you!" "Thank God you're here!"

When your guests depart, escort them to their car or walk along with them until they are safely on their way.

Blessing

(When your guests arrive, hosts say)

ברוכים הבאים!

Brukhim ha'ba'im!

Blessed are you who have arrived!

(Guests reply)

ברוכים הנמצאים!

Brukhim ha'nimtza'im!

Blessed are you who are already here!

(When your guests depart, hosts say)

צאתכם לשלום!

Tzeitkhem l'shalom!

May our guests arrive home safely and in peace.

Teaching

A person should greet a friend with God's name.
As it says, "And behold Boaz came from Bethlehem
and he said to the reapers, 'The Lord be with you!'
And they answered, 'The Lord bless you!'"

(*Jerusalem Talmud:* Brakhot 9:5)

To walk in all God's ways.

(*Deuteronomy 11:22*)

These are the ways of the Holy One: "Gracious and compassionate…" This means that just as God is gracious and compassionate, you too must be gracious and compassionate.

(Sifre Deuteronomy, Ekev)

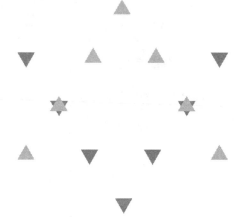

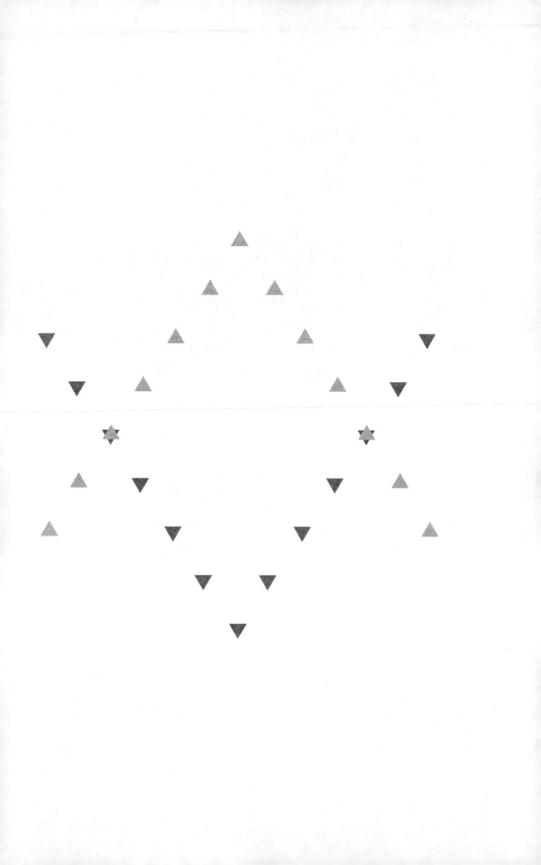

BLESSING ONE'S HOSTS

There is a debate concerning the visitors that came to Abraham and Sarah's tent that day. Were they men or angels? Messengers or prophets? We don't know for sure, but this we know: Sarah baked bread for the visitors and Abraham served them a hearty meal. They were good hosts. The visitors blessed the couple, telling them that their dreams (of a child) would be fulfilled.

הרחמן הוא יברך את בעל הבית הזה ואת בעלת הבית הזה

Harachaman hu y'varekh et ba'al habayit hazeh, v'et ba'alat habayit hazeh

May God bless our hosts

Meditation

Source of Blessing: May our hosts be honored and successful in all that they create and do.

Ritual

Before leaving, shower your hosts with blessings and share with them your best wishes. Describe the feast they prepared for you; recall the different ways they made you feel welcome. Through your attention to all the details, acknowledge the generosity of their time, their resources, their energy, and their affection.

Blessing

(It is customary for guests to lead grace and recite this
blessing for the hosts)

הרחמן הוא יברך את בעל הבית הזה,
ואת בעלת הבית הזה,
אותם ואת ביתם ואת כל אשר להם כמו
שנתברכו אבותינו ואמותינו בכל מכל כל,
כן יברך אותנו כלנו יחד בברכה שלמה ונאמר,
אמן.

*Harachaman hu y'varckh et ba'al habayit hazeh, v'et
ba'alat habayit hazeh, otam v'et beitam v'et kol asher
lahem k'mo she'nitbarkhu avoteinu v'imoteinu bakol
mikol kol, ken y'varekh otanu kulanu yachad
b'vrakhah shleimah v'nomar, Amen.*

Merciful One, bless our hosts and all that is precious to them
just as You blessed our ancestors in every way. Bless us all
with a perfect blessing, Amen.

Teaching

Our rabbis taught, "The host breaks bread and the
guest says grace. The host breaks bread in order to
do so generously, and the guest says the blessing
after the meal in order to bless the host. How does
the guest bless the host? 'May it be God's will that
our host should never be ashamed in this world
nor disgraced in the next world.'"

(*Babylonian Talmud:* Brakhot 46a)

SPECIAL MOMENTS

CELEBRATING A PRIVATE MIRACLE

While Jews everywhere celebrate the national miracles of Chanukah or Purim, individual Jewish communities and families have long had a tradition of re-

מודים אנחנו

Modim anachnu

We thank You for the miracles we celebrate each day

calling particular miracles that have happened just to them. These private miracle days are called "Days of Thanks" or "*Purim Katan*," Special Purims.

Meditation

מודים אנחנו.

Modim anachnu.

We thank You for the miracles we celebrate each day
and for the wonders of every season and every moment.

Ritual

At the Shabbat table, before *kiddush*, invite people to share a private miracle that happened to them in the past week.

You may deepen your awareness of a private miracle that you wish to mark by creating a *brakhah*, a blessing that affirms, "Yes! I know how fortunate I have been, again and again." Your *brakhah* can explain how the miracle has enriched or altered your life, led you from vulnerability to strength, opened your eyes and heart.

Blessing

(After you have told the story of your private miracle)

ברוך אתה שעשה לי נס.

Barukh atah she'asah li nes.

I bless You for this miracle You have given me.

(After you say this blessing, try to recall other miracles with which
you and the people you love have been blessed in the past.)

Teaching

May a people recite a blessing at places where miracles occurred to their ancestors or their teachers?

(Jerusalem Talmud: Brakhot 9:1)

There was once a man who was traveling through
the valley of Aravot. He was thirsty, and a well was
miraculously created for him. Another time, he was
traveling through Machoza when a wild camel
attacked him, and at that moment the walls of a
house collapsed to form a hideout and he escaped
inside. From then on, whenever he came to Aravot
he would say, "Blessed are You who caused the
miracles of the well in Aravot and the miracle of
the camel in Machoza." When he passed through
Machoza, he would say, "Blessed are You who
caused the miracles of the camel in Machoza and
the well in Aravot."

(Adapted from Babylonian Talmud: Brakhot 54a)

CELEBRATING BIRTHDAYS

The world has a birthday on Rosh Hashanah. The trees have a birthday on Tu B'Shevat. On my birthday, I declare a holy day, a day to celebrate my uniqueness, my connection to all that is born, and the completion of another year.

עד מאה ועשרים

Ad me'ah v'esrim

May you live until
one hundred and twenty

Meditation

May this coming year be filled with health, happiness, kindness, peace, growth, and learning.

Ritual

Light the candles on your birthday cake with people you love. As you light each candle, recall a specific blessing of this past year. Blow out the candles! *Yom huledet same'ach!* Happy birthday!

Blessing

(Your loved ones say)

מזל טוב!

Mazel tov!

May you look forward to a good and blessed year.

(You say)

Blessed are You who has sustained me for another year and who
provides me with opportunities to begin anew.

(All say)

הרחמן הוא יחדש עלינו
את השנה הזאת לטובה ולברכה.

*Harachaman hu y'chadeish aleinu et hashanah hazot
l'tovah v'livrakhah.*

May the Merciful One renew this year for goodness and
for a blessing.

Teaching

The older scholars grow, the more wisdom they
acquire, for it is said, "With age comes wisdom,
and with length of days, understanding."

(Babylonian Talmud: Shabbat 152a)

Teach me to number my days so I may develop a
heart of wisdom.

(Psalms 90:12)

HEARING GOOD NEWS

How automatically our words celebrate the blessing of hearing good news. "Oh my God!" we say. "Thank God!" "I can't believe it!" Later, with more deliberation, more reflection, our hearts and minds acknowledge the Divine Source of Blessing that our words so readily locate.

דשנת בשמן ראשי,
כוסי רויה

Dishanta va'shemen roshi; kosi r'vayah

You anoint my head with oil; my cup overflows

Meditation

Whoever says the blessing over a full cup is given
an inheritance without bounds, as it says in Zechariah,
"And full with the blessing of the Lord, you shall
possess the sea and the south."

(Babylonian Talmud: Brakhot 51a)

Ritual

Alone, or with people who celebrate your good news,
fill a beautiful cup with wine or grape juice, letting it
overflow into the saucer below. This is the cup of abundant blessing. Raise it up, fixing your eyes on it. After
the blessing, share your cup with those who share your
good news.

Blessing

כּוֹס יְשׁוּעוֹת אֶשָּׂא וּבְשֵׁם ה' אֶקְרָא.
בָּרוּךְ אַתָּה ה' אֱלֹקֵינוּ מֶלֶךְ הָעוֹלָם בּוֹרֵא פְּרִי הַגָּפֶן.

*Kos yeshuot esah, u'v'sheim Adonai ekra. Barukh atah
Adonai eloheinu melekh ha'olam borei pri hagafen.*

I raise the cup of abundant blessing and invoke the name of
God. Blessed are You, Sovereign of the World, who created
the fruit of the vine.

בָּרוּךְ אַתָּה הַטּוֹב וְהַמֵּטִיב.

Barukh atah hatov v'ha'meitiv.

Thank God for this good news. *L'chaim!*

Teaching

Why did the rabbis connect their discussion of the
blessing we say for good news with their discussion of the blessing we say for rain? "Because hearing good news is like cold water to a thirsty soul."

(Jerusalem Talmud: Brakhot 9:2)

You have changed my grief into dancing! You have
taken off my sackcloth and dressed me with celebration.

(Psalms 30:12)

BEING A GUEST AT A WEDDING

Watching a friend or relative stand under the *chuppah*, we get teary-eyed. We feel as if all of us joined here are entering into a timeless space, a Garden of Eden, a place where magical transition will take place. We, who are guests, need to be here: we are witnesses to love as it transforms into commitment—now and forever.

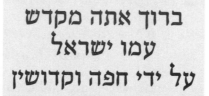

ברוך אתה מקדש
עמו ישראל
על ידי חפה וקדושין

*Barukh atah m'kadesh
amo Yisrael al y'dei
chuppah v'kiddushin*

Blessed are You who
sanctifies us by the sacred
commitment of this
marriage

Meditation

We are all made holy by the commitment of marriage. Loving couples help us to understand that our lives exist in relationships, in sacred bonds that link lovers to families, to community, and beyond.

Ritual

As you search for a present for the couple, look for something they'll need that can also represent an enduring spiritual presence, a witness to the commitment of their love. Write a note to the couple explaining how your present symbolizes your hope to help them build upon and sustain their love. As the couple approaches the *chuppah*, bless them in your heart and imagine specific ways that you can be as fully present for them in the future as you are now.

Blessing

(To be recited as you watch the couple walk down the aisle)

מִי בָרוּךְ עַל הַכֹּל יְבָרֵךְ חָתָן וְכַלָּה.
מִי בָרוּךְ עַל הַכֹּל יְבָרֵךְ אֶת הַקְּהִילָה.

Mi barukh al ha'kol y'varekh chatan v'kallah. Mi barukh al ha'kol y'varekh et ha'kehillah.

May the One who is blessed above all bless this bride and this groom. May the One who is blessed above all bless all of us who witness and pledge to support this sacred commitment.

בָּרוּךְ אֱלֹקֵינוּ שֶׁהַשִּׂמְחָה בִּמְעוֹנוֹ.

Barukh eloheinu she'hasimchah bimono.

In the company of all the wonderful people present, let us bless God who invites us to witness and create this joyous celebration.

Teaching

It is good manners that everyone who partakes of a wedding feast should give a present to the couple.

(Zohar 1:149a)

Rav Ashi said: "One is rewarded for attending a wedding, for saying words to the bridegroom about the bride that bring him joy."

(*Babylonian Talmud:* Brakhot 6b)

SEEING NATURAL WONDERS

We had seen spectacular mountains in the Alps and the Rockies in Colorado. We didn't think Yosemite would be much different. More mountains, maybe some waterfalls, we thought, and it will all be nice— at least we'll get out of the city. Driving from San Francisco through the dry heat of the desert, we pulled into the heart of Yosemite as the sun began to set. We got out of the car and were astounded. What we saw were trees five times bigger than any we'd ever seen, spectacular rocks climbing to the heavens, waterfalls cascading into lush valleys. We were struck silent.

ברוך אתה שככה
לו בעולמו

Barukh atah she'kakhah lo b'olamo

Praised are You who has created such beauty in Your world

Meditation

The world is God's intensely holy place. Hear God's voice in the waters, in the thunder. Hear God's voice in the tall trees, in the forest, in the wilderness.

קול ה' בכח קול ה' בהדר.

Kol Adonai ba'ko'ach, kol Adonai be'hadar.

Hear God's voice in power; hear God's voice in beauty.

(Adapted from Psalms 29:4)

Ritual

In silence, take off (or imagine taking off) your shoes, allowing your feet to touch the ground. As you witness the majestic beauty of high mountains, vast deserts, sunrises, lightning, and shooting stars, take as much time as you need to acknowledge that you stand on holy ground.

Blessing

ברוך אתה עשה מעשה בראשית.

Barukh atah oseh ma'aseh v'reishit.

Praised are You, Renewer of the works of creation. Let me be attentive to the wonder of Your world.

הללוהו שמש וירח. הללוהו כל כוכבי אור.

Halleluhu shemesh v'yarei'ach. Halleluhu kol kokhvei or.

Praised is God, sun and moon. Praised is God, all bright stars.

(Psalms 148:3)

Teaching

And God called the dry places "earth," and the water-springs God called "seas," and God saw that it was good.

(Genesis 1:10)

The skies will rejoice, the earth vibrate with celebration, the sea roar with its full force, the fields sing
out, the trees of the forest cry out in ecstasy.

(Psalms 96:11–12)

Every blade of grass has a guardian above it.

(Zohar 1:34a)

On seeing mountains, hills, seas, rivers, and deserts,
one should say, "Blessed is the One who creates."

(Jerusalem Talmud: Brakhot 9:1)

STANDING AT A CROSSROADS

We reach the moment when a difficult decision needs to be made: some call it a crossroads, some call it a fork in the road. Although we recognize that we are fortunate to have options and opportunities, we know that making a choice or finalizing a decision is a humbling experience, especially when so much seems to depend on it.

וְהָאֵר עֵינֵינוּ

V'ha'eir eineinu

Illuminate us

Meditation

It is a blessing to be in a position to make a choice, one that feels so important, as if it could change my whole life. Remind me to take the time I need, and lead me to make the wiser choice.

Each path has its story, its promises. Help me choose a path of greater light, greater love, and greater life.

Ritual

As you make your umpteenth "pro and con" list before your final decision, pause to remember:

דרכיה דרכי נעם וכל נתיבותיה שלום.

D'rakhe'ha darkhei noam, v'khol n'tivotehah shalom.

The ways of the tree of life are pleasant, and its many different paths lead to peace.

Blessing

ברוך אתה המאיר לעולם כלו בכבודו.

Barukh atah ha'me'ir la'olam kulo b'khvodo.

I bless You as You illuminate my whole world.

הושע ה' את עמך
בכל פרשת העבור
יהיו צרכיהם לפניך.

*Hosha Adonai et amekha b'khol parashat ha'ibur
y'hiyu tzarkhei'hem l'fanekha.*

At each crossroad, may my needs be known to You.

(Adapted from Jerusalem Talmud: Brakhot 4:4)

Teaching

Tamar was told, "Your father-in-law is coming up to Timnah for the sheepshearing." So she took off her widow's garb, covered her face with a veil and, wrapping herself up, sat down at the entrance to Einaim (the place of opened eyes), which is at the crossroads to Timnah; for she saw that Shelah was grown up, yet she had not been given to him as a wife.

(Genesis 38:13–14)

But Moses said to God, "Who am I that I should go to Pharaoh and free the Israelites from Egypt?" And God said, "I will be with you."

(Exodus 3:11–12)

See: today I set before you life and prosperity, death and adversity…. Choose life.

(Deuteronomy 30:15,19)

Many plans are in our minds, but it is God's plan that is accomplished.

(Proverbs 19:21)

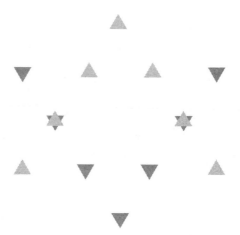

RUNNING A MARATHON

Before a marathon, in the hours immediately preceding the start, I need to concentrate, focusing all my energy and my awareness. During the first two-thirds of the race, I need to let my mind wander. During the final, very tough miles, concentration once again becomes overwhelmingly important. Throughout, I recite *brakhot*, making me attentive to my mind, body, and soul. (Of course, not all of us run marathons, but many of us engage in other challenging activities that feel like marathons, for they stretch us to our limits and even beyond.)

הנותן ליעף כח

Ha'notein la'ya'eif ko'ach

You give strength to the exhausted

Meditation

If my foot slips, Your love supports me.

If I am challenged, You comfort me, soothing my soul.

You pressed me hard,

I nearly fell;

but God helped me.

God is my strength and might,

God has become my deliverance....

Open the gates of victory for me that

I may enter them and praise the Lord.

(Adapted from Psalms 118)

Ritual

As you approach each phase of the marathon, take the time to reflect upon the focus that each blessing provides.

Blessing

(As you wake up before dawn in order to get to the starting line
on time and perform your pre-race rituals)

ברוך אתה ה׳ אלקינו מלך העולם
אשר נתן לשכוי בינה להבחין בין יום ובין לילה.

*Barukh atah Adonai eloheinu melekh ha'olam asher
natan la'sekhvi vina l'havchin bein yom u'vein la'ylah.*

You abound in blessings, giving creatures the
ability to distinguish between day and night.

(As you dress for the marathon)

ברוך אתה ה׳ אלקינו מלך העולם מלביש ערומים.

*Barukh atah Adonai eloheinu melekh ha'olam malbish
arumim.*

You abound in blessings, dressing the naked.

(As you complete your preparations, warming up your body and
providing it with "fuel")

ברוך אתה ה׳ אלקינו מלך העולם המכין מצעדי גבר.

*Barukh atah Adonai eloheinu melekh ha'olam
ha'meichin mitzadei gaver.*

You abound in blessings, preparing a person's steps.

(As you "hit the wall")

ברוך אתה ה' אלקינו מלך העולם הנותן ליעף כח.

Barukh atah Adonai eloheinu melekh ha'olam,
ha'notein la'ya'eif ko'ach.

You abound in blessings, giving strength to the exhausted.

Teaching

Bless God, celebrate God's praises, who has given us life and has not let our feet slip.

(Psalms 66:9)

My help comes from the Lord, Maker of heaven and earth. God will not let your foot give way; your guardian will not slumber.

(Psalms 121:2–3)

NOTICING A CHANGE IN THE SEASONS

There are times when the natural world calls out to us to notice a change. The first chill in the evening air, the first shoots of bulbs, or even the first time we feel the heat of the sun as it awakens us to the yearly cycles of life. In these moments, we are given a preview to the sights, smells, sounds, tastes, and emotions that the new season will bring to us.

מחליף זמנים
משנה עתים

*Machalif z'manim
m'shaneh itim*

You turn the seasons and change the times

Meditation

These will never again cease: sowing time and harvest time, cold and heat, summer and winter, day and night.

(Genesis 8:22)

May this new season bring with it all the familiar memories of past seasons and its own unanticipated discoveries.

Ritual

On noticing signs that indicate a forthcoming change in the season or on sensing one of the season's special sights, smells, sounds, tastes, and feelings, savor it. Reflect on your memory of this time in years past and articulate your hopes for what this new season might bring.

Blessing

(When you first notice a change in seasons)

ברוך אתה הנותן לאדם בינה להבחין בין עת ובין עת.

Barukh atah ha'notein l'adam binah l'havchin bein eyt u'vein eyt.

Blessed are You who grants us the ability to notice the changing seasons.

(On enjoying one of the season's special sights, smells, sounds, tastes, and feelings)

ברוך אתה שככה לו בעולמו להתנאות בהם בני אדם.

Barukh atah she'kakhah lo b'olamo l'hitna'ot bahem b'nei adam.

Blessed are You who has such special things in Your world for people to enjoy.

Teaching

If one goes abroad in springtime and sees the trees sprouting, one should say, "Blessed are You who has not left Your world lacking in anything and has created splendid creatures and trees for all people to enjoy."

(Bablyonian Talmud: Brakhot 43b)

Just as a work of art reflects the genius of the
artist, so the wondrous diversity of living things
reflects the power of God, the miraculous source
of life and beauty. This leads us to a teaching of
Isaiah: Lift your eyes up high and see who created
these things (Isaiah 40:26). Someone studying
Torah who says: "How fine is that tree that God has
created" does not interrupt one's study, but continues it through the admiration of nature.

(CLAL Faculty)

MOVING INTO A NEW HOUSE

After you have moved in and unpacked your boxes, invite family and friends, old and new, to join you for a *chanukat habayit*, a dedication of your new house.

To those unfamiliar with this beautiful practice, explain that this is the Jewish way of transforming a new house into the sacred space of home.

ברוכים הבאים

Brukhim ha'ba'im

We bless those who enter

Meditation

Across this threshold
may these things never cross:
anger and anxiety,
hatred and hunger,
insult and injury.
May this mezuzah,
as we kiss it going in and out,
remind all who enter
to bring with them only
love and laughter,
praise and prayer,
kindness and comfort.
Let the doors of this house be wide open,
so all who enter may find shelter and love.

Ritual

After everyone has assembled, greet your guests with a blessing of welcome. If weather permits, gather just outside your front door. Ask everyone to take a moment to silently meditate upon the blessings they wish for this home.

Sing: *Hinei mah tov u'mah na'im shevet achim gam yachad.*

How very good it is to be together in this house.

Affix the mezuzah, one you have selected because its shape or design is meaningful to you. Hang it on the right side of your doorpost, with the top tilted inward, and say the blessings. Invite everyone to enter your home and, after you have said the blessing for bread, dip your bread in various symbolic condiments, alone or in combinations: salt (symbolizing a life of holiness), oil (sustenance), or honey (sweetness).

As you conclude, offer a blessing of thanksgiving. Invite your guests to share their blessings for your new home.

Blessing

(As you bless your guests)

ברוכים הבאים בשם ה'.

Brukhim ha'ba'im b'sheim Adonai.

We bless all who come in God's name with
love and peace to help us make this house our Jewish home.

(Recite the blessing for installing a mezuzah)

ברוך אתה ה׳ אלקינו מלך העולם
אשר קדשנו במצותיו וצונו לקבוע מזוזה.

Barukh atah Adonai eloheinu melekh ha'olam asher kidshanu b'mitzvotav v'tzivanu likbo'a mezuzah.

Blessed are You, Gracious One, our God, Sovereign of all worlds, who makes us holy with Your *mitzvot* and commands us to affix the mezuzah.

ברוך אתה ה׳ אלקינו מלך העולם
שהחינו וקימנו והגיענו לזמן הזה.

Barukh atah Adonai eloheinu melekh ha'olam shehecheyanu v'kiy'manu v'higi'anu lazman hazeh.

Blessed are You who has kept us in life, sustained us, and enabled us to reach this season.

(Before you eat the bread)

ברוך אתה ה׳ אלקינו מלך העולם המוציא
לחם מן הארץ.

Barukh atah Adonai eloheinu melekh ha'olam ha'motzi lechem min ha'aretz.

Blessed are You, our God, who sustains us with bread from the earth.

Teaching

And you shall write them upon the doorposts
(*mezuzot*) of your house and upon your gates.

(Deuteronomy 6:9)

The mezuzah, in addition to marking the passage
from public to private domain, also designates
that the private domain must be a certain type of
dwelling, one that is fit for human living. When we
mark our doorpost with a mezuzah, we are reminded that our domain must be a fitting abode for an
image of God, such as ourselves.

(CLAL Faculty)

JOINING A SYNAGOGUE

Joining for the first time. Moving to a new community. Switching from one synagogue to another. Whatever your reason, becoming a member of a synagogue is a commitment— certainly of money, usually of time, and often of emotion. It is literally a defining moment, defining who you are as a Jew and as a member of a movement, deepening your connection to a community and to the entire Jewish people.

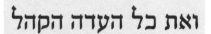

ואת כל העדה הקהל

V'et kol ha'aydah hak'heil

And assemble the whole congregation

Meditation

Compile a list of some or all of the reasons you have joined this particular synagogue. Here are some possibilities:

Prayer and spiritual growth

Children's education

Adult learning

Lifecycle events (birth, bar and bat mitzvah, marriage…)

Community

Commitment

Friendship and shmoozing

Social action

Rabbi

As your eyes rest on each reason you've listed, imagine what you hope to receive from the synagogue and the kinds of roles you or your family might play in this new community.

Ritual

Arrange to deliver your first dues (or whatever act or item signals membership in the synagogue) in person. Ask if the rabbi or one of the leaders of the synagogue, volunteer or professional, can be present. Express to them your hopes for what your membership might mean for you and for your family, and what you, in turn, can bring to the congregation—and right away, volunteer to do something, anything! The best way to feel part of a congregation is to roll up your sleeves and contribute your gifts to keep it vital.

Blessing

(Rabbi or synagogue leader says)

מי ששכן את שמו בבית הזה,
הוא ישכין ביניכם אהבה ואחוה ושלום וריעות.

Mi shc'shikein et shmo babayit hazeh, hu yashkin beyneichem ahavah v'achvah v'shalom v'reiut.

May the One who lets God's name dwell in this house let love, fellowship, peace, and friendship dwell.

(*Babylonian Talmud:* Brakhot 12a)

(New congregant replies)

ברוך אתה ה' אלקינו מלך העולם
שהחינו וקימנו והגיענו לזמן הזה.

Barukh atah Adonai eloheinu melekh ha'olam shehecheyanu v'kiy'manu v'higi'anu lazman hazeh.

Blessed are You who has kept us in life, sustained us, and enabled us to reach this season.

Teaching

The Lord said to me, "Assemble the people for Me,
and I will let them hear My words, so that they
may learn to hold Me in awe as long as they live
on the earth, and may teach their children so."

(Deuteronomy 4:10)

One way to express what you hope this new community will offer you and what you will bring to
it is to contribute a book to the synagogue library.
Choose a book that reflects your own Jewish journey as one way of bringing more of who you are
into this new community.

(CLAL Faculty)

TAKING ON A JEWISH NAME

We have a Jewish tradition of having "both a civil name, one we reserve for worldly pursuits, and a Jewish name, one by which we are called in the holy community of Israel," according to Rabbi Arnold Stiebel of Woodland Hills, California. Yet many Jews, both adults and children, do not know their Jewish names or have never received one. Rabbi Stiebel invites people in his community to discover their lost Hebrew names or to choose a new name at an annual consecration service held at Chanukah time (the holiday of dedication), in which they formally take on their Jewish name and explain what it means or why they selected it. In taking the time to discover or select a Jewish name, we affirm the Jewish identity we are embracing.

ברוך השם

Barukh ha'shem

Blessed is the name

Meditation

We all have three names: one given by our parents, one we're called by our friends, and one we call or think of ourselves. May I fully become the Jewish name by which I am called.

Ritual

At a consecration service on the Shabbat of Chanukah, people taking on new or reconsecrated names are invited up to the *bimah* before the open ark to have their Jewish name "officially" bestowed upon them and to have the opportunity to explain the meaning of their name.

One can also choose to hold a home ceremony when taking on a Jewish name. In this more intimate setting, it is possible to share the stories behind the name and to explain what it means personally.

Blessing

(Those who witness your taking on your new name)

May you be called in Israel _____ .
    May your name be a blessing.

Teaching

You shall no longer be called Abram, but your
name shall be Abraham, for I make you the father
of a multitude of nations.

(Genesis 17:5)

And God said to Abraham, "As for your wife Sarai,
you shall not call her Sarai, but her name shall be
Sarah. I will bless her indeed."

(Genesis: 17:15–16)

The name of the righteous is a blessing.

(Proverbs 10:7)

A good name is better than riches.

(Proverbs 22:1)

People will call you by the name that is rightfully yours.

(Adapted from Babylonian Talmud: Yoma 38a)

In the Judeo-Spanish tradition…when the child is
given a name which is the same name as that of
some of the persons present, those bearing the
name…are given a slap by all the others who are
present at the ceremony…to alert them to the fact

that their attributes, which were developed as a
result of the special combination of their name and
soul, will now be shared by a new member of the
House of Israel.

(*Herbert Dobrinsky,* A Treasury of Sephardic
Laws and Customs)

WEARING A *TALLIT* FOR THE FIRST TIME

Before we had palm pilots, we remembered things with strings. Like the string tied around a finger, the fringes of the *tallit* (called *tzitzit*) are reminders. As Moses instructed us so long ago, "And you will look at the strings, and you will remember all the instructions of God…and you will be holy." Wrapped in the *tallit*, its fringes dangling from each of its four corners, we remember our sacred missions—to fix the world, to seek justice, and to pursue peace—and we feel protected by the many memories woven within its threads.

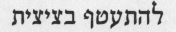

להתעטף בציצית

L'hitateif ba'tzitzit

To wear the sacred fringes

Meditation

וארשתיך לי לעולם.

V'eirastikh li l'olam.

Encircle me with Your covenant. Wrap me in Your light.

Ritual

Carefully unfold the *tallit*. Grasp the *atarah*, the long strip of cloth that contains the blessing or embroidered design, and that will lay against your neck. Hold the *tallit* stretched out before you. Recite the blessing, then lift your right hand over your left shoulder, wrapping the *tallit* around you. If it is a large *tallit*, you may wish to toss the *tzitzit*, the fringes, to both sides. Adjust the *tallit* so that it hangs equally over both shoulders.

Blessing

ברוך אתה ה׳ אלקינו מלך העולם
אשר קדשנו במצותיו וצונו להתעטף בציצית.

*Barukh atah Adonai eloheinu melekh ha'olam asher
kidshanu b'mitzvotav v'tzivanu l'hitateif ba'tzitzit.*

Blessed is the Holy One, whose *mitzvot* make our lives holy and
who gave us the *mitzvah* to wrap ourselves in *tzitzit*.

ברוך אתה ה׳ אלקינו מלך העולם
שהחינו וקימנו והגיענו לזמן הזה.

*Barukh atah Adonai eloheinu melekh ha'olam
shehecheyanu v'kiy'manu v'higi'anu lazman hazeh.*

Blessed are You who has kept us in life, sustained us,
and enabled us to reach this season.

Teaching

Let all my being praise the Lord who is clothed
in splendor and majesty, wrapped in light as in a
garment, unfolding the heavens like a curtain.

(Adapted from Psalms 104)

Like paratroopers who always take their parachutes
with them when they jump from planes, those who
have begun wearing a *tallit* as they pray discover
just how essential it is. As a parachute catches the
breath of the wind, protecting those who dare to
jump into the air, the *tallit* ensures God's embrace
for those who dare to leap into prayer.

(CLAL Faculty)

RETIRING

How can we experience retirement as a period of life with creative potential, an opportunity to do things we haven't had time for or things we've only dreamed about? Rabbi Irving (Yitz) Greenberg suggests we be guided by the *mitzvah* of *la'erev* (doing it again). "Middle age and old age are a time to create again, espe-cially so in this generation as the human life span increases.... People who create again, who break new ground as they grow, make a further major contribution to the increase of life.... In the process, they keep their own lives vital."

ארך ימים אשביעהו

*Orekh yamim
asbi'eyhu*

Blessed with a full life

Meditation

So teach us to number our days, that we may gain a heart of wisdom.

(Psalms 90:12)

In my retirement, may I be granted opportunities to love, to learn, and to make the world a better place. May I be blessed with health, contentment, and companionship.

Ritual

As you plan for retirement, seek role models for the kind of retirement you desire: the person who learns a new skill or hobby; the former business executive who takes time to tutor young protégés; the community leader who continues to find new ways to grow and contribute; the man or woman who seizes the opportunity to deepen relation-ships with friends and loved ones. Keep their stories with you as you embark upon this new part of life.

Blessing

(On the day you embark upon your new life)

הקדוש ברוך הוא.

Ha'kadosh barukh hu.

Blessed is the One who grants us success in our endeavors.

Teaching

In the morning sow your seed, and at evening do not let your hands be idle, because you do not know which is going to succeed.

(Ecclesiastes 11:6)

At fifty—the age of counsel…at eighty—the age of strength.

(Pirkei Avot 5:24)

Gray hair is a crown of glory, to be found in the path of righteousness.

(Pirkei Avot 6:8)

An elderly and wise woman once gave me some excellent advice: "Aaron," she said, "it is very important as you get older to engage in an activity that you didn't engage in when you were very young, so that you are not continually in competition with yourself as a young man."

(Aaron Copland, The New Music 1900–1969)

HEALING

PRAYING FOR HEALING

What can we say when we join together to pray for those who are sick? What can we say at a board or committee meeting, at services or in any group setting when we become aware of those who cannot be with us because they are sick? We know that there is more to healing than tests, procedures, medicines, medical professionals, and hospitals. We know that prayer and reaching out are sources of healing, for ourselves and for others.

כִּי אֵל מֶלֶךְ רוֹפֵא
נֶאֱמָן וְרַחֲמָן אַתָּה

*Ki el melekh rofei
ne'eman v'rachaman
atah*

For You are the faithful
and merciful God of
healing

Meditation

אֵל נָא רְפָא נָא לָהּ.

El na r'fa na lah.

Please, God, bring healing.

Ritual

When you become aware of members of your community who are ill, share this prayer of healing and find specific ways in which different individuals can be of help to the ill and their families.

Blessing

מִי שֶׁבֵּרַךְ אֲבוֹתֵינוּ וְאִמּוֹתֵנוּ יְבָרֵךְ אֶת (הַחוֹלִים הָאֵלֶּה)
וְיָבִיא עֲלֵיהֶם רְפוּאַת הַנֶּפֶשׁ וּרְפוּאַת הַגּוּף
יַחַד עִם כָּל חוֹלֵי עַמּוֹ יִשְׂרָאֵל.
בָּרוּךְ אַתָּה ה' רוֹפֵא חוֹלִים.

Mi shebeirakh avoteinu v'imoteinu yevarekh et [name
those who are ill] *v'yavi aleihem r'fuat ha'nefesh
u'r'fuat ha'guf yachad im kol cholei amo Yisrael.
Barukh atah Adonai rofei cholim.*

May the One who was a source of blessing for our ancestors bring
blessings of healing upon [name those who are ill], a healing of
body and a healing of spirit. May they be healed along with all
those who are in need. Blessed are You, Source of Healing.

Teaching

כִּי אֵל מֶלֶךְ רוֹפֵא נֶאֱמָן וְרַחֲמָן אָתָּה.

*Ki el melekh rofei ne'eman
v'rachaman atah.*

For You are the faithful and merciful
God of healing.

(Amidah)

בָּרוּךְ אַתָּה ה' רוֹפֵא חוֹלֵי עַמּוֹ יִשְׂרָאֵל.

Barukh atah Adonai rofei cholei amo Yisrael.

Praised are You, Healer of Your people Israel.

(Amidah)

VISITING THE SICK

As I approach this obligation, this mitzvah of bikkur cholim, I hope I may provide comfort and strength. Let me enter the room with respect for the dignity and infinite uniqueness of the one whom I encoun- ter, a *tzelem elohim*, an image of God. May I see that image at this moment. May I shed any anxiety or fear that I feel as I enter the room. May I move *karov*—closer—and not distance my body or my heart.

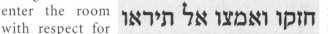

חזקו ואמצו אל תיראו

*Chizku v'imtzu,
al ti'ra'u*

Be strong and have
courage, fear not

Meditation

(Before entering the room of one who is ill)

הנני מוכן ומזומן.

Hin'ni mukhan u'm'zuman.

Here I stand, ready and waiting, to fulfill the *mitzvah* of *bikkur cholim*, to strengthen those who are sick.

מה אני בורא עולמות ומחיה מתים אף אתם כן.

Mah ani boreh olamot u'm'chayeh meitim af atem ken.

Just as God creates worlds and inspires life, you, human beings, are also capable of doing the same.

(Midrash Psalms 116:8)

יהיו לרצון אמרי פי והגיון לבי לפניך.

Yi'h'yu l'ratzon imrei fi v'hegyon libi l'fanekha.

May the words of my mouth and the meditations of my heart be sources of healing.

Ritual

As you visit, focus on your potential to bring light, wholeness, and connection to the one who is ill. Search for the many ways you can bring healing: holding hands, offering interesting news, singing a song, celebrating Shabbat or a holiday, telling a joke.

Blessing

Walk in the ways of God. As God visits and brings comfort to those who are ill, so must I emulate God by visiting and bringing comfort to those who are sick.

(Adapted from Babylonian Talmud: Sotah 14a)

(As you end your visit, say aloud or in your heart)

ברוך אתה ה' רופא חולי עמו ישראל.

Barukh atah Adonai rofei cholei amo Yisrael.

Blessed is the One who heals the sick.

Teaching

Rabbi Charles Savenor tells this story: When he was studying hospital chaplaincy he witnessed his supervisor, a Protestant minister named Mary, say to the patient she visited, "I would like to say a prayer for you. What do you hope for, Harry? Come, let us hold hands, focus our energy and pray together." From her lips emanated a prayer as eloquent as a psalm. This short, spontaneous prayer included the person's name, vocalized the patient's hopes for a speedy recovery, and requested strength for the patient's family. "Dear God, I am here with Harry from Long Beach. Harry is scared, Lord. He has a wife and two daughters. He wants to recover and return home in one piece, able to work on their behalf and to serve You. Please allow this man the chance to heal and to feel whole again. Amen." Later, when Rabbi Savenor visited his own father who was ill, he prayed: "*Mishebeirakh*: May God, who grants life and vitality to all creations, bestow upon me the strength to work with the ill and empower me to facilitate in the healing of others. God, I love my father and I want him to live. Please, please keep an eye on him. Amen."

(Hadassah *Magazine, January 1998*)

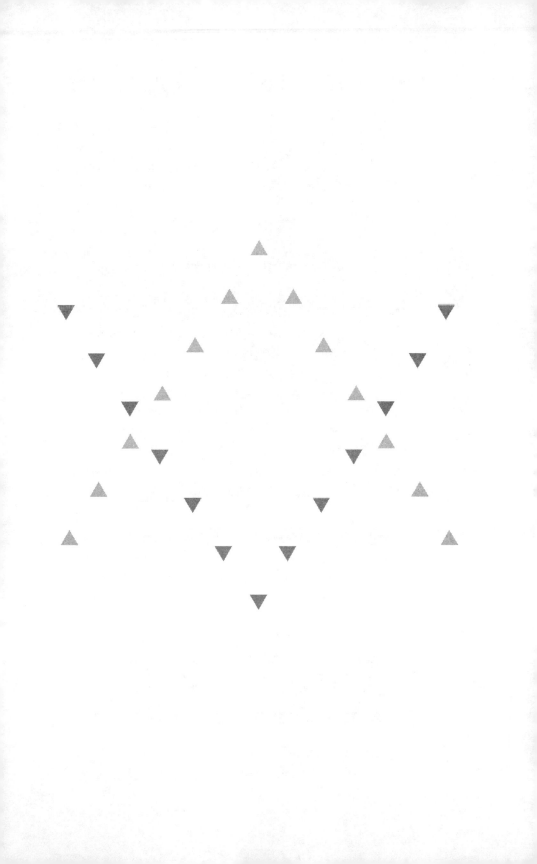

FINDING HOPE IN A TIME OF ILLNESS

In the course of an illness, there are moments when treatment moves us toward health, or when an unexpected course of events gives us hope. There are also moments when having a good day, or a slightly bet-ter day, is cause enough to rejoice. At these times, we become grate-fully aware of the wonders of the most basic functions of the human body. In such moments, we take the oppor-tunity to offer thanksgiving.

הרופא לשבורי לב

Ha'rofei l'shvurei lev

God heals our brokenness

Meditation

May all those who are ill be blessed with the strength and patience to reach moments of gratitude.

Ritual

Gather with those who have supported you through your illness. They might be family members, friends, and health care professionals. After telling the story of your journey toward healing, recite the following blessing.

Blessing

ברוך אתה ה' אלקינו מלך העולם הגומל לחיבים טובות שגמלני כל טוב.

Barukh atah Adonai eloheinu melekh ha'olam ha'gomel le'chayavim tovot she'g'malani kol tov.

Praised are You, my God, Ruler of the Universe, who grants goodness beyond expectation, who has blessed me with all that is good.

(Those present respond)

מִי שֶׁגְּמָלְךָ כָּל טוֹב הוּא יִגְמָלְךָ כָּל טוֹב סֶלָה.

Mi she'g'malkha [for males] *she'g'malekh* [for females]
kol tov, hu y'gmalkha [for males] *yigm'lekh* [for
females] *kol tov selah.*

May God continue to bless you with all that is good.

Teaching

From my narrow place, God, I called out, and You
answered me with infinite expansiveness. Open the
gates, and I will pass through them.

(Adapted from Psalms)

After Rabbi Judah had recovered from illness, he
was visited by a group of his colleagues. When they
saw him, they said: "Blessed be the Compassionate
One, who has sustained you!" They waited for
Rabbi Judah to elaborate on the blessing, but
instead he simply said, "Amen." The visitors were
shocked by his short reply. Sensing their confusion,
Rabbi Judah taught, "Just by saying 'amen' to your
prayer, I have offered a thanksgiving to God!"

(Adapted from Babylonian Talmud: Brakhot 54b)

Joy is the great healer!

(Rabbi Nachman of Bratzlav)

TREATING A PATIENT

You have created me in Your image and blessed me with the capacity and the opportunity to be a healer. Like You, I do not heal alone. You have imbued me with a desire to learn and have blessed me with teachers whose wisdom I have acquired. You have inspired those who came before me to create miraculous healing tools that I now can use for good. You sur-round me with all those who support the healing work to which I dedicate my life. Help me to see my patients as covenantal part-ners, help me to open my eyes to see each patient I meet as a whole human being. May I extend the dignity and quality of my patients' lives and honor their uniqueness and infinite value.

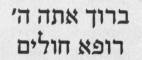

ברוך אתה ה'
רופא חולים

*Barukh atah Adonai
rofei cholim*

Blessed are You, Source
of Healing

Meditation

Help me to bring healing to my patients even as I accept, with humility, the finite quality of life. Let me be alto-gether present to my patients.

Ritual

(For all those who are involved in healing)

Pause before encountering a patient. Acknowledge how you are joined in your healing work by the Divine Presence, the *Shekhinah*, resting at the head of the bed.

Blessing

(To be said before treating a patient or initiating any
medical procedure)

רפאנו ה' ונרפא הושיענו ונושעה כי תהלתנו אתה
והעלה רפואה שלמה לכל מכותינו כי אל מלך
רופא נאמן ורחמן אתה. ברוך אתה ה' רופא חולים.

*R'fa'einu Adonai v'neirafei, hoshi'einu v'nivashe'ah, ki
l'hilulelnu atah. V'ha'aleih r'fuah shleimah l'khol
makoteinu, ki el melekh rofei ne'eman v'rachaman
atah. Barukh atah Adonai rofei cholim.*

Heal us, Source of Healing, and we shall be healed. Save us and
we shall be saved, for You are our song. Bring to us a healing of
mind, heart, and body, from all that hurts us, for You are a true
and compassionate healer.

Blessed are You who sends Raphael, the messenger of healing, to
guide my hand and my mind to care for Your creations.

(*Adapted from the* Amidah)

Teaching

Oh, God on High. As I begin this holy work of
healing the human beings you have created, I
place myself before You. Give me courage, energy,
and passion so I may do my work in faith. Let my
desire for a good reputation not blind me from
seeing Your presence. Allow me to encounter each
patient who comes to me as an image of God,

without differentiating between rich and poor, ally or enemy, good or evil. When I see human beings in pain, show me their humanity. If physicians wiser than I wish to teach me, let me learn from them, for the Torah of medicine is vast. Dear merciful God, give me strength, courage and spirit, so that I may watch over life and healing.

*(Adapted from the "Prayer for the Doctor,"
attributed to Maimonides)*

STARTING TO WORK OUT

Maybe it was your own idea to begin exercising (again). Maybe your doctor advised you to exercise. Either way, you've made what you hope to be a sacred commitment, a commitment to a full and healthy life. You're going to keep that commitment today, and the next day, and the next…

ברוך אתה המכין
מצעדי גבר

*Barukh atah
ha'meikhin mitzadei
gaver*

Blessed are You who
guides us in our path

Meditation

Each extra step on the treadmill or the Stairmaster, each lap in the pool or around the track, each turn of the pedal, each lift of the weights, each stretch of muscles long out of use… in each bead of sweat and panting breath I praise You—

בכל עצמותי

b'khol atzmotai
with all my bones—

for allowing my body to affirm life.
    Teach me discipline, encourage me to take good care of the body You have given me.

כל עצמותי תאמרנה ה' מי כמוך?

Kol atzmotai to'marnah Adonai mi khamokha?

With all my bones I cry out, "Who is like You, God?"

(Psalms 35:10)

Ritual

As you climb, step, run, swim, stretch…pause to feel
your body affirming your commitment to choose life.
Select words of a psalm or liturgical passage to
repeat in your mind as you work out. For example:

אלקי נשמה שנתת בי טהורה היא.

Elohai neshamah she'natata bi t'horah hi.

My God, the spirit You have given me is pure.

Blessing

(Each time you begin to work out)

ברוך אתה אשר ברא את האדם בחכמה.

Barukh atah asher bara et ha'adam b'chokhmah.

Blessed are You who has created the human body in wisdom.

(As you begin this new training program)

ברוך אתה אוזר ישראל בגבורה.

Barukh atah ozer Yisrael bigvurah.

Blessed are You who girds me with strength.

(When you join a new gym or acquire new athletic equipment)

ברוך אתה שעשה לי כל צרכי.

Barukh atah she'asah li kol tzorki.

Blessed are You who has provided for all my needs.

(When you have completed your workout)

ברוך אתה הנותן ליעף כח.

Barukh atah ha'notein la'ya'eif ko'ach.

Blessed are You who restores me.

Teaching

Since the body's good health and physical perfection are divine qualities, it is impossible to comprehend God when one is afflicted with illness; therefore, one must distance oneself from things that harm the body and conduct oneself in ways that lead to health.

(*Maimonides,* Mishneh Torah, *Laws of Knowledge 4:1*)

Not as much as the synagogue or house of study, perhaps, the gym is nevertheless also a place for the pursuit of the holy. God has given us bodies to keep and use, and the good that our bodies can do will be brought about only if we work to keep them healthy. Thus it is our responsibility, to the extent possible, to stay in shape. Saying a *brakhah* before getting on the treadmill would be fully appropriate.

(*CLAL Faculty*)

QUITTING SMOKING

A Hasidic tale is told: Rabbi Isaac Vorecki once woke up in the middle of the night with an urge for a pinch of snuff. He reached across his bedside table for the box, which was just beyond his grasp. "Should I get out of bed and get it?" he thought to himself. He began to debate the matter in his mind: "If I don't get out of bed when I need something, I'll become lazy! But if I take a pinch of snuff, then I'll be giving in to my cravings!" So the rabbi made the following vow: "I will get up and get the box, but I will resist my impulse to take a pinch!"

מתיר אסורים

Matir asurim

Who frees the captives

(Yalkut Sippurim)

Meditation

כל הנשמה תהלל יה הללויה.

Kol ha'neshama tehallel Yah, Halleluyah!

Let all my breath sing Hallelujah!

(Psalms 150)

Like Your rainbow, each breath I take is the sign of a covenant I shall try to honor.

May I succeed as I try to quit smoking, so I can care for my body.

Ritual

Smoking is a physical addiction, and withdrawal is physically and psychologically challenging. As Jewish tradition teaches that we must keep connected to our community, make efforts to create the community of support around you that you will need and reach out to your supporters when you need them.

Blessing

ברוך אתה ה׳ אלקינו מלך העולם מתיר אסורים.

Barukh atah Adonai eloheinu melekh ha'olam
matir asurim.

Blessed is the One who frees those who are held captive.

Teaching

Who is heroic? Those who try to master
their desires.

(Pirkei Avot 4:1)

Hold fast to discipline, do not let go; keep it, it
is your life.

(Proverbs 4:13)

How small is the mind which is ruled by desire,
and how great is the one ruled by the soul!

(Israel Salanter, Iggeret HaMusar)

Quitting smoking is an accomplishment, but it is a
loss as well. We smokers know there is a close connection between our personalities and our smoking.
We turn to smoking for comfort; it brings us relief
from tension at anxious moments. For when we
give up smoking, we give up an aspect of ourselves
and change who we are. That's scary.

(CLAL Faculty)

CREATING OPPORTUNITIES, OPENING DOORS

When one door closes, or so the maxim goes, another door opens. In retrospect, many of us have seen that this is indeed the case in our lives: the loss of one opportunity or the blocking of one path does indeed open up new, unimagined, and some-times altogether better possibilities. When we strain to see the opportunities before us, how shall we move away from the constricting place of closing doors and move toward liberating new vistas where we can seek or create opening doors?

פתחו לי שערי צדק
אבא בם

Pitchu li sha'arei tzedek avo vam

Open the gates of *tzedek* and I will enter

Meditation

You have taken us from slavery to freedom, from sorrow to joy, from mourning to festivity, from thick darkness to great light, from enslavement to redemption.

Ritual

Make one small gesture each day that might bring you even slightly closer to a new and open door. Write one letter, make one phone call, initiate a conversation, consider one alternative approach, step outside and take a different route.

Blessing

(As you make each gesture that brings you closer to a new
open door, say)

Blessed is the One who helps me keep my eyes open to the out-
stretched arms (zero'a netuyah) and the signs (otot), divine and
human, that will lead me to a place of promise.

מודה אני לפניך...שהחזרת בי נשמתי בחמלה...

Modeh [for males] *Modah* [for females] *ani
l'fanekha...she'hechezarta bi nishmati b'chemlah.*

I am grateful as my spirit returns to me.

Teaching

A time to weep and a time to laugh,
A time to lament and a time to dance for joy...
A time to seek and a time to give up,
A time to keep and a time to throw away.

(Ecclesiastes 3:4,6)

פתחו לי שערי צדק אבא בם.

Pitchu li sha'arei tzedek avo vam.

Open the gates of *tzedek* and I will enter.

(Psalms 118:19)

LIFE AND DEATH

HEARING OF A DEATH

First there is shock, then a silence that sinks in and wraps itself around the heart. Then, there comes a moment when the grief begins to grope for sound: it is *kriah*, the tearing of cloth.

ברוך דין האמת

Barukh dayan ha'emet

Blessed is the Judge of Truth

Meditation

In our tradition, mourners tear their clothing *(kriah)*, either upon hearing about a death or at the time of burial. The tearing of cloth: what a powerful image. Cloth is made from numerous strands of flimsy threads that become strong when woven together. Such is human life—each one of us, alone, is like a thin thread, easily broken and able to support only a tiny portion of the weight of the world. Woven together, in family, friendship, and community, our strength is multiplied and enhanced. Yet, when a person dies, a hole is torn in the weave and the fabric can unravel. Just one person, one thread....

Ritual

Kriah: As our hearts are torn, so we tear our clothing.
(When the period of mourning comes to an end, some
mend the clothes they have torn and donate them to
charity; others wear them on the *yahrzeit*, or anniversary
of a death, as a remembrance.)

Blessing

(Even upon hearing bad news, the worst news of all, we still bless
God. The blessing is defiant and counterintuitive. We affirm that
love and hope still need to endure and that life still makes sense.)

ברוך אתה ה׳ אלקינו מלך העולם דין האמת.

*Barukh atah Adonai eloheinu melekh ha'olam dayan
ha'emet.*

Praised are You, Judge of Truth.

Teaching

Jacob rent his clothes, put sackcloth on his loins,
and observed mourning for his son many days. All
his sons and daughters sought to comfort him, but
he refused to be comforted.

(Genesis 37:34–35)

Saul and his son Jonathan are dead…. David took
hold of his clothes and rent them, as did all who
were with him. They mourned and wept, and they
fasted until evening for Saul and his son Jonathan.

(2 Samuel 1)

MAKING A *SHIVA* CALL

When we make a *shiva* call, we sometimes worry, "What shall I say?" We remind ourselves, "Trust and be patient.

המקום ינחם אתכם

Ha'makom y'nacheim etkhem

May God comfort you

The right words—which may be no words at all, just a rich, holding silence—will come from our hearts."

Meditation

Dear God, help me to ease the pain of those who mourn by letting them know that my heart is breaking along with theirs. May my presence lessen their loneliness and bring comfort.

Ritual

(When you make a *shiva* call)

Let the mourners initiate the conversation. Let them choose what you will talk about, or let them choose silence. You may want to ask to hear stories about the person who has died or you can tell a story that would honor him or her. You are not expected to stay too long. Often, a brief visit is fine. As you leave, you may wish to speak the ancient wise words, "May God comfort you among the mourners of Zion and Jerusalem," or more simply, "May you be comforted."

(When you make a *shiva* call from a distance)

In an ideal world, a *shiva* call should be made in person. If that is impossible, you can still be present and share your grief and concern by phone, letter, or e-mail. The *ikar*, the essential thing, is the connection, the reaching out. The following story is told: On November 21, 1997, the *New York Times* reported that Dr. Leonard Wexler, a pediatric oncologist, comforted the parents of nineteen-year-old Jonathan Eisman, who had died of cancer, saying, "I hope that there can be some solace for you, as there was for me, in knowing that you raised a wonderful, caring, funny, charming son who touched the lives of everyone he met and made them better for having known him." The doctor did not say these words in his office or on the telephone, Esther B. Fein reported. Rather, "Dr. Wexler's gentle words sped from his computer terminal in upper Manhattan to that of the Eismans in Wayne, New Jersey, and in that flash of cyber-connection, a human heart was eased."

Blessing

המקום ינחם אתכם בתוך שאר אבלי ציון וירושלים.

Ha'makom y'nacheim etkhem b'tokh sh'ar aveilei tziyon vi'Yerushalayim.

May God comfort you among the mourners of
Zion and Jerusalem.

תנחמו מן השמים.

Tinachamu min hashamayim.

May your comfort come from heaven.

Teaching

Moses said to the Lord: "Please, O Lord, I have never been a man of words…" and the Lord said…"Who gives speech?…Is it not I?…Now go, and I will be with you as you speak."

(Exodus 4:10–12)

REMEMBERING THE LOSS OF SOMEONE YOU LOVE

Words cannot always provide comfort after the loss of a loved one. Each year, on the *yahrzeit*, or anniversary of someone's death, we light a candle, perform acts of lovingkindness, and teach some of the wisdom of the person we remember.

נר ה' נשמת האדם

Ner Adonai nishmat ha'adam

The light of God is the soul of the human being

Meditation

Lighting this *yahrzeit* candle is a small thing we do to honor you—to say how much you mean to us, to say we remember you, to say we love you. May you feel all our love, every moment of every one of the other days of the year…and may you be in peace.

Ritual

At the *yahrzeit*, alone or with members of your family who join together in remembrance, light a *yahrzeit* candle or candle that can safely burn for many hours. You may wish to place photos or objects nearby that will kindle your memory and help you tell the story of this life to others. Recall the person's wisdom. This might have been family wisdom; folk wisdom; Torah wisdom; scholarly, artistic, culinary, or mechanical wisdom. Theirs may have been the wisdom of being fully present at the times when we most needed them. Quietly, we reflect on the legacy of their lives, mourning the uniqueness that is now lost. If some of their gifts have been passed on to us, we do the things they would be doing. We tell stories, make their roast chicken, listen to favorite albums, walk trails, knit socks, fix bicycles, do an act of *tzedakah*, keeping alive the wisdom that we have inherited and embraced.

Blessing
(Upon lighting a candle)

יזכר אלקים נשמת _____.

Yizkor eluhim nishmat _____.

May God remember the soul of _____.

In loving tribute to [his or her] life, I will study and perform acts
of lovingkindness.
Through study and deeds, and through prayer and memory,
may [his or her] soul be bound up in the bond of life, a source of
endless blessing.

(As you recall the person you love)

Direct my heart toward God and toward the memory of
_____ , and may I be comforted. May [his or her]
memory inspire me to live justly and kindly.

ברוך אתה המנחם בזכרונות.

Barukh atah ha'menacheim b'zikhronot.

Blessed are You who comforts us with memories.

Teaching

אשר בידך פקדון כל רוחות.

Asher b'yadekha pikdon kol ruchot.

In Your hand is the safekeeping of all spirits: You
would not erase our memories.

(Tziduk Hadin)

ברוך אתה...זוכר חסדי אבות.

Barukh atah...zokheir chasdei avot.

Blessed are You...who recalls the deeds
of our ancestors.

(Amidah)

In American tradition, we remember people on the
anniversary of their birth: George Washington's
birthday, Abraham Lincoln's, Martin Luther King,
Jr.'s. Yet in Jewish tradition, we remember people
we have loved on the anniversary of their death,
their *yahrzeit*. We remember the fullness of a life,
from beginning to end. The candle we light is the
light of their memory, which has no end.

(CLAL Faculty)

MOVING OUT OF MOURNING AND BACK INTO LIFE

There are many customs associated with *shiva*, the period of mourning, that mourners can perform, such as covering mirrors, not greeting or being greeted by visitors, and allowing others to prepare food. These customs are designed to free mourners from worldly concerns while they are preoccupied in grief. When *shiva* ends, the mourners leave their house and walk around the block. The first step out the door symbolizes the return to the larger world outside home, which had been a holding place for wounded hearts. The mourners may now be greeted and begin to resume normal daily activities.

שלום עליכם

Shalom aleikhem

May you know wholeness and peace

Meditation

Help me to feel comforted. Help me to return to the world by greeting all whom I meet with "Shalom" (wholeness and peace) and wishing them "Shalom" as we depart. Eternal One whose name is peace, grant my heart healing and shalom.

עושה שלום במרומיו הוא יעשה שלום
עלינו ועל כל ישראל ואמרו אמן.

Oseh shalom bimromav hu ya'aseh shalom aleinu v'al kol Yisrael v'imru amen.

May the One who grants peace and wholeness above, grant peace and wholeness upon us and upon all Israel, and let us say Amen.

Ritual

At the conclusion of *shiva*, it is time to leave your house and walk around the block. Returning back home does not mean that mourning and being comforted are over, but it does signify that the time has come to restore connections to a living world and to begin to seek healing of one's broken heart. Greet all those you encounter, both while walking and on returning home, with "Shalom," symbolizing your hope for increasing peace and wholeness in the days and weeks to come.

Blessing
(Returning home)

Blessed is the One who comforts me, who deepens the memories of my loved one, and who helps me return to life.

Teaching

Your lovingkindness sustains the living.

(Amidah)

Your sun will not go down again, your moon will not depart; for the Eternal One will be your light forever, and your days of mourning ended.

(Isaiah 60:20)

When the others rise to say *kaddish*, I also rise, but I stand silent. I am with them, but I am not of them. I am a mourner on his way out of mourning, a man in the halfway house of grief, whose release from death's company has at last been granted.

(Leon Wieseltier, Kaddish)

WRITING AN ETHICAL WILL

The lessons we teach can live on after us. In writing an ethical will, a traditional Jewish practice, we can spell out the values that we hope our loved ones will embody in their lives. One day this intimate letter will pass into the hands of those we leave behind. In the meantime, writing it will remind us of those values by which we strive to live.

זוכר חסדי אבות

Zokheir chasdei avot

You remember the ethical example of our ancestors

Meditation

Help me to express the deepest and most important values that I seek to embody in my own life and to transmit to my loved ones. When the time comes, may my loved ones receive my words, and may they be sustained and strengthened on their lifelong journeys.

Ritual

Set aside some private time, taking a few minutes to center yourself. Reflect upon the sacred purpose that is at hand.

Begin composing your ethical will. (You can write, tape, or video it.) These questions can help you get started: What are the important things you have learned in life? What traits do you admire most in others? What important work have you begun that you hope your descendants can complete?

You need not finish the ethical will in a single session. You can redo or revise it as the years pass. Feel free to reread it from time to time, drawing strength of purpose from it. It is, after all, your own ethical mission statement.

When complete, place your ethical will with your most important papers. You might want to attach it to your legal will so it will be found at the proper time.

Blessing

(When you have composed your ethical will)

Blessed is the One who enables me to express the ideals that are my life and my soul.

Teaching

The best thing for you, my children, is to serve God from your heart, without falsehood or shame.

(Gluckel of Hameln)

At my grave, and throughout the whole year, and then every year on the anniversary of my death, my remaining son and my sons-in-law, if they are so inclined, should say *kaddish* for me. And if they do not wish to do this, or if it is against their religious convictions, they may fulfill their obligation to me by assembling together with my daughters and grandchildren and good friends to read this testament, and also to select one of my stories, one of the really merry ones, and read it aloud in whatever language they understand best, and let my name rather be remembered by them with laughter than not at all.

(Sholom Aleichem)

SAYING GOOD-BYE TO A BELOVED PET

When we must say good-bye to a beloved pet, the loss feels so painful. Although we know that losing a pet is not the same as losing a human being, it is still a real loss, and we need to mourn. Finding a loving way to say good-bye to a pet is a sensitive way to reaffirm the infinite value of life and of love.

לֵךְ לְשָׁלוֹם

Lekh l'shalom

May you go in peace

Meditation

You blessed our days with love and companionship. We will never forget you.

Ritual

Find an appropriate place to bury the pet—in the yard, in the countryside, or in a place set aside for burying animals. If the pet is small, find an appropriately sized box and place it inside. Find a stone or make a marker for the place where your pet will be buried. As the burial takes place, anyone who wishes can tell stories and share special memories of the pet.

    If it is not practical for you to bury your pet, you can still set aside a time for telling stories and sharing memories. You might want to do this at a particular place, inside or out, that your pet loved best.

Blessing

(After you have told your stories and shared your memories)

ברוך אתה שלא חסר בעולמו דבר.

Barukh atah she'lo chisar b'olamo davar.

Blessed are You in whose world nothing is lacking; it is filled
with wonderful animals that bring joy and companionship to
human beings.

Teaching

And God made all kinds of animals, wild beasts
and animals of every kind, and all kinds of crawl-
ing animals that are on the earth. And God saw
that this was good.

(Genesis 1:25)

But God paid attention to Noah and all the living
things, all the animals that were with them in the
ark, and God brought a wind across the earth, and
the waters abated.

(Genesis 8:1)

Even the sparrow has found a home, and the swal-
low a nest for herself in which to set her young
near Your altar, O Lord....

(Psalms 84:4)

LEARNING

STARTING SCHOOL

As each of our children neared the end of summer vacation before starting school for the first time, they sensed that a new stage of life lay ahead. Before, there was no homework; now there would be. Before school felt like play; now it might feel like work. To start them off on their very important journey, we developed rituals to ease the transition. Together, we packed away swimsuits, shovels, and sunscreen and set out the equipment that had been carefully selected for the upcoming journey—the backpack, the notebooks. Finally, we performed the new school year ritual that has become traditional in our family: The child received his own alarm clock, because now he's "big enough" to wake up on his own.

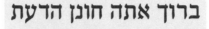

ברוך אתה חונן הדעת

Barukh atah chonen ha'da'at

Blessed are You who bestows wisdom

Meditation

Teach us to use all of our days so our hearts will be full.

(Psalms 90:12)

Ritual

On the evening before the first day of school, put away the things of summer and collect all the new equipment for school, placing it carefully in a very special backpack. (Don't forget a note saying "I love you!")

Blessing

(For parents, grandparents, and children, the night before
school starts)

Blessed are You, Eternal God, who makes us holy with *mitzvot*
and commands us to search for, gather, and prepare all that we
need in order to learn.

ברוך אתה שעשה לי כל צרכי.

Barukh atah she'asah li kol tzorki.

Blessed are You who provides me with all I need.

Teaching

בן חמש למקרא.

Ben chameish la'mikra.

At the age of five, serious study begins.

(Pirkei Avot 5:24)

Your teachings are precious...they live forever. For
our ancestors, for us, for our children, for every
generation, for all ages from the first to the last.
Your teachings are true, everlasting.

(Morning prayer)

BEGINNING TO STUDY TORAH FOR THE FIRST TIME

In medieval Europe, a Jewish boy would be wrapped in a *tallit*, carried to his teacher's house, and be seated on the teacher's lap. His teacher would recite the Hebrew alphabet, written on a tablet, and would instruct the child to lick the honey that had been smeared on the tablet. Today, it is we who create the sweet memories that our daughters and sons will have when they look back and recall their first encounter with Torah.

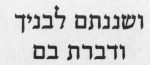

ושננתם לבניך
ודברת בם

*V'shinantam l'vanekha
v'dibarta bam*

You shall teach these
words diligently to your
children

Meditation

May learning Torah be a source of joy for our children.
Help them to learn easily, to perform Your *mitzvot*, and
to be open to wisdom and insight. May we support
them as they wrestle, discover, challenge, and delight.
May we watch them blossom in their learning.

Ritual

Together with your child, spend time selecting and decorating a special backpack just for Torah studies. Before it
is used the first time, fill it with treats that delight your
child. On the first day of your child's Jewish studies, as
you stand at the threshold of your child's classroom,
place your hands on your child's head and give your

child traditional and personal blessings. You can begin by saying, "This is my hope as you begin your studies: _____ ."

If you or another adult in your family is beginning or intensifying your own Torah studies, invite people you love to bless you and celebrate with delicious sweets.

Blessing

(As you stand outside your child's classroom)

והערב נא ה' אלקינו את דברי תורתך
בפינו ובפי עמך בית ישראל
ונהיה אנחנו וצאצאינו
וצאצאי עמך בית ישראל כלנו
יודעי שמך ולומדי תורתך לשמה.
ברוך אתה ה' המלמד תורה לעמו ישראל.

V'ha'arev na Adonai eloheinu et divrei toratkha b'finu u'v'fi amkha beit Yisrael, v'nih'yeh anachnu v'tze'etza'einu, v'tze'etza'ei amkha beit Yisrael, kulanu yod'ei sh'mekha v'lomdei toratekha l'shma. Barukh atah Adonai, ha'm'lamed torah l'amo Yisrael.

Holy One, may the words of Your wisdom be pleasant in our mouths and in the mouths of Your people, the house of Israel, so that we and our children may all know You and study Your wisdom. Blessed are You who teaches us wisdom.

(All who begin Torah studies)

ברוך אתה ה׳ אלקינו מלך העולם אשר בחר בנו מכל
העמים ונתן לנו את תורתו. ברוך אתה ה׳ נותן התורה.

*Barukh atah Adonai eloheinu melekh ha'olam, asher
bachar banu mi'kol ha'amim, v'natan lanu et Torato.
Barukh atah Adonai, notein ha'Torah.*

Blessed are You who has chosen us from all peoples by giving us
Your Torah. Blessed are You for the gift of Torah.

Teaching

Creator of the World! We know that You
have created the world with great wisdom.
We have urged our child to study the Torah
with dedication. I beseech You, God, strengthen
our child to learn with ease, to heed Your
mitzvot and our advice. Lead our child in the
path of Torah and *mitzvot*. Amen.

(*"A Tkhine for a Mother Who Leads Her Child to Kheyder"*
in The Merit of Our Mothers: A Bilingual Anthology of
Jewish Women's Prayers, *Tracy Guren Klirs, ed.*)

Educate children in the way to go, and when they
are old, they will not depart from it.

(*Proverbs 22:6*)

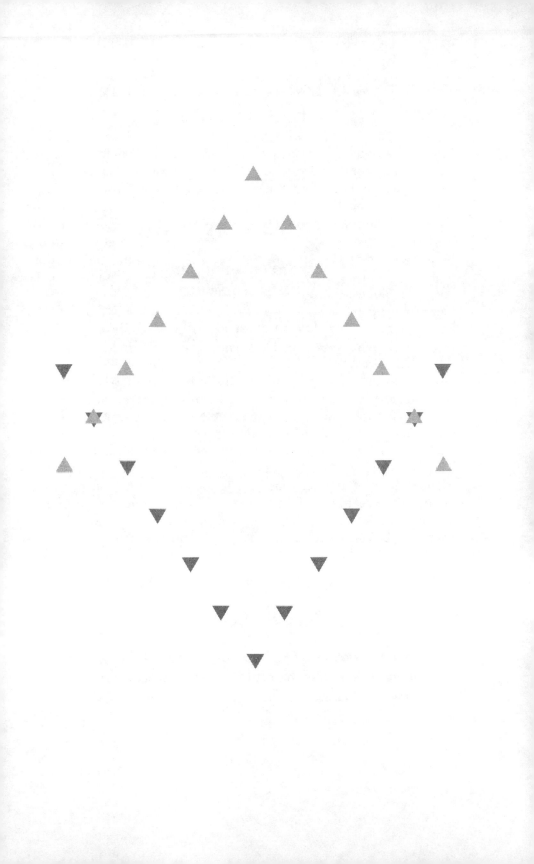

STUDYING SACRED TEXTS EACH DAY

Daf Yomi, a page a day. There are groups all around the world that study a page of Talmud each day, usually in the morning before work, over lunch in offices, or at night on home-bound commuter trains. Some groups study the *parsha*, the Torah por-tion, each week, meeting on an evening after the children are asleep, or meeting on Sabbath afternoons to study with the same group of friends, year after year. Some study Torah just with a *hevruta*, a study mate, whom they meet at a set time or on the fly, sharing both Torah learning and secrets of the soul. Some do their Torah learning in

והאר עינינו בתורתך

*V'ha'eir ei'nei'nu
b'Toratekha*

May Torah study fill our
eyes and saturate our lives

cyberspace, with a virtual teacher, a virtual class or a virtual *hevruta*. And there are those of us who prefer studying Torah alone. We might be study-ing the tradition-al sacred texts, but we may also be finding our sources of Torah in less traditional places: in novels, in books of philosophy, in great volumes of art or photographs, and in the wisdom teaching of other faiths. We may find Torah at the movies, in museums, on city streets, and in nature. We may find Torah in reflecting on our lives. All of this is the study of Torah, understood by Jews as a height-ened form of worship.

Meditation

May my study be a source of life, wisdom, healing, and kindness. May I learn deeply and share what's moved me with others.

Ritual

Before and after you engage in sacred learning, take
a moment to separate yourself from what you have
just been doing and what you will do afterwards. Allow
the study of deep teachings to transform you, and bless
others by sharing what you have learned in ways they
can grasp.

Blessing

Blessed is the One who commands us to immerse ourselves
in Torah each day.

Teaching

When ten people sit together and occupy themselves with Torah, the *Shekhinah*, God's presence,
resides among them. The same applies to five...and
to three...and to two.... And how can it be shown
that the same applies even to one? Because it is
said, "In every place where I cause My name to be
remembered, I will come to you and bless you."

(Pirkei Avot 3:7)

When you study Torah God speaks to you; when
you pray you speak to God.

(Moral Grandeur and Spiritual Audacity, *Abraham Joshua
Heschel; edited by Susannah Heschel*)

Unlike printed Bibles in Hebrew or in translation,
the real Torah is made without vowels. All you
have in front of you are consonants. Read as it
appears, Torah is gibberish. It only makes sense

when a reader—you—interact with it. You have to
provide the vowels. You do this by reading the text
aloud. You do this by adding your breath to the
printed letters. Just as God breathed life into Adam,
so you breathe life into Torah. The interaction of
you and the text makes the text your personal reve-
lation. Tradition says that each Jew received her
own Torah at Sinai. When you read Torah yourself
you are receiving your own personal Torah.

(Rami Shapiro,"Simply Simchat Torah," SimplyJewish.com)

FINISHING AN IMPORTANT BOOK

You have just finished reading a book that has made a huge impression on you. It might be a novel, a collection of poetry, or a scholarly study; it might be a book of Torah, rabbinic commentary, or Jewish history. One thing you know for sure: this book has changed your life. Maybe it has helped you to understand something you never understood before; maybe it has given you access to feelings you didn't know were possible. This is the kind of book you will return to, for you know that it has more to teach you. You can't stop there, however; you want to share the book with people you care about because this book could change their lives as well.

הדרן עלך

Hadran alakh

We shall return to You

Meditation

I've got to share this book with others! Help me to communicate how important this book has been to me and, hopefully, how important it could be for them.

Ritual

The urge to share a book that has changed your life is so great—so give in to it! It's no wonder that a *siyyum*, the Jewish ceremony held to celebrate finishing the study of a sacred book, involves inviting friends and family to come together to hear a section of the work read aloud. If the book that has meant so much to you is a paperback, purchase a few copies of it and share it with people whom it will touch. Or photocopy a few passages, enough to intrigue them to read the rest. Inscribe the books or copies, explaining why this book has meant so much to you, how it has changed your life, and why you think it could have special meaning for the people to whom you're sending it. You might even want to mark a particular place that struck you.

Blessing

(As you send off your books or copies)

I bless the Source of Wisdom who grants me the ability to read and understand. I am grateful for this great book and for being able to grow through its teachings. May I return to this beloved book, and may I return to it in the company of those who will share it with me.

Teaching

May good come to me, because whenever I see a scholar complete a tractate, I declare it a holiday for all who learn.

(Babylonian Talmud: Shabbat *118b–119a)*

Torah that is studied for its own merit *(Torah lishmah)* is a Torah of lovingkindness, whereas Torah that is studied for an ulterior motive is not a Torah of lovingkindness. And some say that Torah which is studied in order to teach is a Torah of lovingkindness.

(Babylonian Talmud: Sukkah *49b)*

HONORING A TEACHER AT THE END OF THE YEAR

It has been said that teachers think they're teaching us what they know, they hope they're teaching us what they believe, but all they can ever really teach us is who they are. At the end of a year of learning with a teacher, we may feel we have learned what we came to learn, we may feel frustrated that we did not master more of the information we sought, we may feel awed by how much there is yet to learn, and we may feel that we have been deeply changed by the experience.

ברוך אתה חונן הדעת

Barukh atah chonen ha'da'at

Blessed is the One who has graced us with intelligence

Meditation

When study had been completed in Rabbi Ammi's
  school, students would say to each other:
May you see your world in your lifetime...
May your eyes sparkle with the light of the Torah,
And your face shine like the brilliance of the heavens.
May you speak words of wisdom, and may the deeds of
  righteousness you do fill your body with joy.
And may your feet hurry to hear the words of the
  Ancient One, who sets the cycles in motion.

(Babylonian Talmud: Brakhot 17a, *adapted from
a translation by Danny Siegel)*

Ritual

We are blessed when we teach what we have learned in the name of the person who taught it to us. Before your classes come to an end, honor your teachers by telling them the "torah" (which means "teaching" or "instruction") that you, in turn, will teach in their name.

Blessing
(As you depart from your teacher)

אתה חונן לאדם דעת ומלמד לאנוש בינה.
חננו מאתך דעה בינה והשכל.
ברוך אתה ה' חונן הדעת.

Atah chonen l'adam da'at um'lamed le'enosh binah.Choneinu mei'itkha dei'ah binah v'haskeil. Barukh atah Adonai chonen ha'da'at.

You graciously endow us with intelligence, teaching wisdom and understanding. Grant us knowledge, discernment, and wisdom. Praised are You, God, who graciously grants intelligence.

(Bless your teacher)

May you be blessed and strengthened as you have blessed and strengthened your student.
May you have peace, grace, kindness, mercy, long life and everything you need.

(*From* Kaddish d'Rabanan)

Teaching

Why are the words of Torah like fire? A fire is built by many logs, and the words of Torah survive only through many minds.

(Adapted from Babylonian Talmud: Ta'anit *7a)*

Rabbi Elazar ben Shamua taught: "The dignity of your students should be as precious to you as your own. The dignity of your colleagues should be as precious to you as your reverence for your teacher. The reverence for your teacher should be as great as your reverence for God."

(Pirkei Avot *4:15*)

LEADERSHIP AND COMMUNAL LIFE

BUILDING A PLURALIST JEWISH COMMUNITY

The old adage "two Jews, three opinions" is a humorous way to address the challenge of bringing Jewish people and diverse communities together. The best tool that we have to bring people together across boundaries is still a shared love for discussion. Through learning and honest intellectual engagement, we affirm that there are many branches on our Tree of Knowledge.

עם ישראל חי

Am Yisrael chai

When we are with each
other, Israel lives

Meditation

A central challenge to our world is to affirm so many strong particular identities within the context of a larger human identity. When we engage in building pluralist communities, unified and guided by diverse interpretations of Torah, we will be an *or la'goyim*, a model for the world.

Learning how to argue about what is most important and appreciating that all our arguments are for the sake of heaven will be crucial if we are to translate our new condition into a vital, rich, and meaningful Judaism, Jewish people, and Jewish culture.

We are challenged to be on the avant-garde of humanity: How remarkable it is to be alive, to be sustained as we sustain each other, and to arrive together at this moment in time, a moment making us all worthy of blessing.

Ritual

(Gather people together in small groups and take time to discuss the meaning of the following essential Jewish concepts)

1. שמע ישראל.

Shma Yisrael.

Listen more and speak less. Hear all the voices that seek to be heard, reflect on the variety of reactions, and diagnose the situation. Help others to do the same. Offer proposals that can incrementally improve the situation.

2. עם אחד בלב אחד.

Am echad b'lev echad.

Affirm: We are one people with one destiny. Know how and where to articulate anger, arguing civilly and lovingly. Listen to the truth of critiques, even when embedded in distracting anger. Become expert in understanding the sources of the anger of those who disagree so you can respond to the root causes.

3. חזק, חזק, ונתחזק.

Chazak, chazak, v'nitchazeik.

Attempt to create change through the political process, and seek political support for your initiatives. If you lose, be gracious.

4. אהבת ישראל.

Ahavat Yisrael.

Be loving, insistent, patient. For our journey to be covenantal, we must be on it together.

Blessing

(As you prepare to study principles of building a pluralist
Jewish community)

Blessed are You who gives us the wisdom to engage in
loving debate.

עַם יִשְׂרָאֵל חַי.

Am Yisrael chai.

When we are with each other, Israel lives. When we are a people
of wrestlers, Israel lives.

Teaching

Every dispute that is for the sake of heaven in the
end will be permanently established. And every
dispute that is not for the sake of heaven in the
end will not be permanently established. What is
an example of a dispute for the sake of heaven?
The dispute between the House of Hillel and the
House of Shammai. What is an example of a
dispute that is not for the sake of heaven? The
dispute of Korach and his followers.

(Pirkei Avot 5:20)

For the building is constructed from various parts,
and the truth of the light of the world will be built
from various dimensions, from various approaches,
for these and those are the words of the living
God…. It is precisely the multiplicity of opinions
that derive from variegated souls and backgrounds

that enriches wisdom and brings about its enlarge-
ment. In the end, all matters will be properly
understood and it will be recognized that it was
impossible for the structure of peace to be built
without those trends that appeared to be in conflict.

(Rabbi Abraham Isaac Kook, Olat Raya, vol. 1, p. 330)

EXAMINING OURSELVES AS LEADERS

You are a leader. In your home, your family, in your community, in a business. You have responsibilities for others. All year long, you are responsible for evaluating whether those you lead are proceeding as they should. On the morning of Yom Kippur, you have the opportunity to "self-correct," to examine yourself and how, in the past year, you might have exercised your leadership differently.

סלח לנו, מחל לנו,
כפר לנו

Slach lanu, m'chal lanu, ka'per lanu

Forgive us, pardon us, grant us atonement

Meditation

Before Aaron, the high priest, can ask for forgiveness for the whole congregation of Israel, he is told to scrutinize himself first. He is to bathe. He is to put on sacred garments. Standing in the *ohel mo'ed*, the tent of meeting, he is to ask for forgiveness for himself. Only then can the circle widen—only then is he prepared to "make expiation for the whole congregation of Israel."

(Leviticus 16)

Ritual

All those who have leadership responsibilities are asked
to come up to the Torah for the third *aliyah* on Yom
Kippur. As you hear the words chanted, you, like Aaron,
have this opportunity to ask for forgiveness for yourself
before you ask for forgiveness for your community.

It is a time for introspection: Where have you, as a
leader, "missed the mark"? What decisions could you
have made as a leader, but did not? Focus: Given all that
you know now, given all of your dreams of a more perfect world, how might you exercise your leadership in a
different way?

NOTE: If group *aliyot* are not the custom in your community, you
may choose to listen to the words of Leviticus 16 as they are
chanted on Yom Kippur and focus on these concerns of leaders.

Blessing

(The person who is called to the Torah)

ברכו את ה׳ המברך.

Barkhu et Adonai hamvorakh.

Blessed are You, Source of Blessing.

(The congregation responds and the leader repeats after them)

ברוך ה׳ המברך לעולם ועד.

Barukh Adonai hamvorakh l'olam va'ed.

Blessed are You, Source of Blessing, forever.

ברוך אתה ה' אלקינו מלך העולם
אשר בחר בנו מכל העמים ונתן לנו את תורתו.
ברוך אתה ה' נותן התורה.

Barukh atah Adonai eloheinu melekh ha'olam asher
bachar banu mi'kol ha'amim v'natan lanu et Torato.
Barukh atah Adonai notein ha'Torah.

Blessed are You, Lord our God, Sovereign of the Universe, who
has chosen us from among all peoples by giving us Your Torah.
Praised are You, Lord, who gives the Torah.

(After the portion is read, the person says)

ברוך אתה ה' אלקינו מלך העולם
אשר נתן לנו תורת אמת וחיי עולם נטע בתוכנו.
ברוך אתה ה' נותן התורה.

Barukh atah Adonai eloheinu melekh ha'olam asher
natan lanu Torat emet v'chayei olam nata b'tocheinu.
Barukh atah Adonai notein ha'Torah.

Blessed are You, Lord our God, Sovereign of the Universe, who
has given us the Torah of truth, planting within us life eternal.
Blessed are You, Lord, who gives the Torah.

Teaching

And Aaron is to bring near the bull for the sin offering that is his, so that he may effect atonement on behalf of *himself* and for his household.... Then he is to slay the hairy goat of the sin offering that is the *people's*.... Thus he shall purge the Shrine of the uncleanness and transgression of the Israelites, whatever their sin. [emphasis added]

(Leviticus 16:6, 15–16)

Here I stand, humbly, trembling in Your presence, pleading on behalf of Your people Israel.... Therefore...I plead for help as I seek mercy for myself and for those whom I represent.... Accept my prayer as the prayer of one uniquely worthy and qualified for this talk.... Draw Your veil of love over all our faults.

(Hineni, *from the High Holiday Service*)

TAKING ON NEW RESPONSIBILITIES

Beginning a new job or taking on new responsibilities is a time for reflection: What are the opportunities, obligations, and responsibilities that your new position offers? What are your initial goals? How does your move to this new job connect to the bigger picture of your life? It is a time for imagination.

ברוך שתחדש עלי
את העסק הזה
לטובה ולברכה

*Barukh she't'chadeish
alai et ha'esek hazeh
l'tovah v'livrakhah*

May the new work I do be
a source of goodness and
blessing

Meditation

Just as the Jews left Egypt and entered Israel in the springtime, my own new beginning reminds me of the blessing of beginning anew, facing different challenges and growing.

As I begin anew, let me rediscover the relationship between what I do and my deep purpose. Source of Blessing, may my new work be a blessing, allowing me to discover and affirm the sacred in every day and realize my full potential.

Ritual

On the day you begin your new work, as you settle into your work space, look for tangible symbols of renewal that will remind you of hopefulness, purpose, vigor, and new chances that your new work may promise. Or you might choose to bring an object that expresses how you can link your new work to your *shlikhut*, your deep purpose.

Blessing

ברוך שתתחדש עלי את העסק הזה לטובה ולברכה.

Barukh she't'chadeish alai et ha'esek hazeh l'tovah v'livrakhah.

May the new work I do be a source of goodness and blessing.

ברוך אתה ה' אלקינו מלך העולם
שהחינו וקימנו והגיענו לזמן הזה.

Barukh atah Adonai eloheinu melekh ha'olam shehecheyanu v'kiy'manu v'higi'anu lazman hazeh.

Blessed are You who has kept us in life, sustained us, and enabled us to reach this season.

Teaching

היום אתם יוצאים בחדש האביב.

Ha'yom atem yotzim b'chodesh ha'aviv.

Today you are leaving in the month of springtime.

(Exodus 13:4)

David was successful in all his undertakings, for the Lord was with him.

(1 Samuel 18:14)

Survey the course you take, and all your ways will prosper.

(Proverbs 4:26)

The very concept of work defined for purposes of Shabbat is modeled on creation, on God's work.

(Irving [Yitz] Greenberg, The Jewish Way)

TAKING ON A VOLUNTEER ROLE

At the Red Sea, the children of Israel stood paralyzed, a great sea before them and the mighty Egyptian army at their backs. It took a brave volunteer, Nachshon, the chief of the tribe of Judah, to wade into the water and show them that the sea would split, just as God and Moses promised. "For that reason the tribe Judah was worthy to be made the ruling power in Israel" (Babylonian Talmud: *Sotah* 37a).

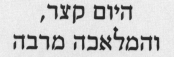

היום קצר,
והמלאכה מרבה

Hayom katzar, v'hamlakhah m'rubah

The day is short, the task is great

Volunteering often feels like that: caught between family and work responsibilities on the one side, and the seemingly endless needs of the less fortunate on the other side. It's not easy to take the plunge.

Meditation

Our sages teach: "You are not required to complete the work, but you are not free to evade it, either."

(Pirkei Avot 2:21)

Ritual

Volunteering is its own ritual: ladling out food at a soup kitchen, organizing a fundraising drive for a neighborhood school, joining the board of a nonprofit organization. Every volunteer act announces to friends, family, and colleagues that you are committed to a better world, as daunting a proposition as that may be. Be a Nachshon—a role model—for others standing on the seashore who, with the slightest nudge, might join you.

Blessing

(On becoming God's partner in the daunting work ahead, say
"Barukh atah" and add one or more of the following phrases that
reflect the responsibilities you will assume)

Blessed are You who:	*Barukh atah:*	:ברוך אתה
• feeds the hungry	• *hazan et ha'kol*	• הזן את הכל
• heals the sick	• *rofei cholim*	• רופא חולים
• clothes the naked	• *malbish arumim*	• מלביש ערומים•
• raises up those who are bowed down	• *zokeif k'fufim*	• זוקף כפופים•
• gives strength to the weary	• *ha'notein la'ya'eif ko'ach*	הנותן ליעף כח•

(From the Morning Blessings)

(On being able to share our prosperity with others)

ברוך אתה שעשה לי כל צרכי.

Barukh atah she'asah li kol tzorki.

Blessed are You who provides me all that I need.

(From the Morning Blessings)

Teaching

You are to follow the ways of the Holy One. God clothed the naked, so should you clothe the naked. The Holy One visited the sick, so should you visit the sick. The Holy One buried the dead, so should you bury the dead. The Holy One comforted mourners, so should you comfort mourners.

(Adapted from Babylonian Talmud: Sotah *14a)*

Describing the volunteer work of Devorah Benjamin, who helps Jewish brides and grooms have festive weddings, Jonathan Mark writes, "Watch through the windows of this small apartment on Montgomery Street. There's Devorah on the phone, surely making arrangements. In the living room, Shmuel talks to a groom-to-be. Perhaps it is for people like this, in every generation, that God Himself made the Israelites His bride under the clouds of that desert mountain."

(The Jewish Week, *April 7, 2000)*

HOLDING A MEETING

In the lot behind my childhood house was a large, untended bush. If we crawled under the first set of branches, we would arrive in a fantastic cavelike area, which we referred to as "the fort." We held meetings in the fort—many meetings in which we beat sticks on the dirt floor, deciding who was the leader and what we stood for and what we were going to do. As an adult, I am still going to meetings, and the discussions are the same—it's the consequences that are larger.

לשם שמים

L'sheim shamayim

In the name of heaven

Meditation

As we prepare for a meeting, let us recall: Each meeting we hold, no matter what the agenda, is an opportunity for sacred encounter and accomplishment, provided we use our creativity, our generosity and our knowledge of Torah to guide us.

Ritual

As your meeting begins, establish these ground rules:

1. Everyone here is a **צלם אלקים**—*tzelem elohim*, created in God's image, being of infinite value, unique and equal. Allow time for everyone to speak. Invite and encourage everyone's participation.

2. We are part of a **ברית**—*brit*, a covenantal relationship. Listen carefully, respectfully, and sympathetically to what others are saying.

3. **אלו ואלו**—*Eilu v'eilu*, all these alternative Jewish views are the living words of the living God. Focus on sharing your own views and experiences and work to gain insight from views other than your own.

Blessing

(When you have set the ground rules)

Blessed are any disagreements which are **לשם שמים**, *l'sheim shamayim*, in the name of heaven, for they will have lasting value.

(Pirkei Avot 5:20)

Teaching

Seven traits characterize...learned people: Learned people do not begin speaking before those who are older or wiser than they are; they do not interrupt when others speak; they do not answer impetuously; they ask relevant questions and reply accurately; they discuss first things first and last things last; they admit their ignorance; they acknowledge the truth.

(Pirkei Avot 5:9)

INSTALLING A NEW COMMUNAL LEADER

When we at CLAL created a ceremony to celebrate the installation of our new chairman of the board, we turned to the rituals of Simchat Torah for inspiration, as they allowed us to start fresh while still sustained by the past.

יברכך ה' וישמרך

*Y'varekh'kha Adonai
v'yishm'rekha*

May God bless you and
keep you

Meditation

With the permission of God, our covenantal partner in
    the work of creation,
And with the permission of the Torah, the source of
    wisdom, which urges us to choose life for our people
    and the world,
And with the permission of the friends gathered here
    today to welcome our new leader,
We promise all the support of our hands and our hearts.
May you succeed in all that you do, and may you lead
    us in wisdom, in righteousness, and in faithfulness.
May your leadership be accounted to you as sacred
    service, and let us say, Amen.
Arise, arise, arise [name] who today accepts upon [himself or herself] the leadership of [name of organization].

Ritual

Call up your new leader and offer the blessing of the community. Select representative members of the community to publicly offer their own personal blessings.

Blessing

(All who are present offer the new leader this blessing)

יברכך ה׳ וישמרך.

Y'varekh'kha Adonai v'yishm'rekha.

God bless you with success and achievement, and keep you from being corrupted, routinized, or hardened by it.

יאר ה׳ פניו אליך ויחנך.

Ya'er Adonai panav eilekha vi'chuneka.

May God show you favor, thereby giving you authority and power, and be gracious to you so that people willingly respond to you, becoming partners.

ישא ה׳ פניו אליו וישם לך שלום.

Yisal Adonai panav eilekha v'yaseim l'kha shalom.

May God turn toward you, showering you with life and joy, and grant you peace, giving you shalom, inner peace, wholeness, completion of yourself, completion of your leadership. Let us say Amen.

Teaching

Now this is the ceremony that you are to make for
them, to hallow them, to serve Me as priests.

(Exodus 29:1)

You shall seek out from among the people
capable people who fear God…set these over
them as leaders.

(Exodus 18:21)

Who knows, perhaps you [Esther] have attained
this royal position for just such a crisis.

(Esther 4:14)

El rey es con la gente.
The King is with the people.

(Ladino Proverb)

CELEBRATING A NEW COMMUNITY BUILDING

How shall we celebrate the sacred space we have worked together to imagine and build? When the holy work of creating the sacred space of the tabernacle, God's dwelling place, the *mishkan*, was completed by all the children of Israel, Moses marveled at their work and offered his blessing.

בית נאמן בישראל

Bayit ne'eman b'Yisrael

A true house of Israel

According to the midrash, these are the words of Moses' blessing: May it be God's will for the Shekhinah, the Divine Presence, to abide in the work of our hands, hearts, and minds and let the graciousness of God be upon us and upon what we have created.

Meditation

All of us here, each in different ways, have participated together in creating this sacred space. Let the doors of this building be wide open, so all may enter to explore, finding shelter, finding ourselves, finding community. May we know God's presence here, and may our care for this building be *avodat ha'kodesh*, sacred work, as we tend to the details of maintaining this building, providing programs that will take place in it, and attending to the people who enter.

Ritual

Call everyone together by blowing a shofar. Tell the story *(maggid)* of how this building came to be. Tell the story of the name it has been given and what it means. Invite all who have come to celebrate the completion of this building. Write down your greatest dreams for this building: all the hopes, visions, and ideals. You might begin this way: This is my hope: _____ . Invite representatives of different parts of the community to share their dreams aloud. Collect all these dreams in a box, and guard them as promises to be kept. Lastly, hang a mezuzah on the doorpost.

Blessing

(Recite the blessing for installing a mezuzah)

ברוך אתה ה' אלקינו מלך העולם
אשר קדשנו במצותיו וצונו לקבוע מזוזה.

Barukh atah Adonai eloheinu melekh ha'olam asher kidshanu b'mitzvotav v'tzivanu likbo'a mezuzah.

Blessed are You, Gracious One, our God, Sovereign of All Worlds, who makes us holy with Your *mitzvot* and commands us to affix the mezuzah.

ברוך אתה ה' אלקינו מלך העולם
שהחינו וקימנו והגיענו לזמן הזה.

Barukh atah Adonai eloheinu melekh ha'olam shehecheyanu v'kiy'manu v'higi'anu lazman hazeh.

Blessed are You who has kept us in life, sustained us, and enabled us to reach this season.

And let them make Me a sanctuary that I may dwell among them.

(Exodus 25:8)

And all the work of creating the *mishkan* was done by the children of Israel. Each part of it was created just as God commanded Moses.

(Exodus 39:32)

May all who enter be blessed in the name of God.

(Psalms 118:26)

And Solomon sent to Hiram saying…"I propose to build a house in the name of God; as God promised my father David, saying, 'Your son…will build a house in My name.'"

(1 Kings 5:19)

NAMING A COMMUNITY

When it comes time to officially name a new synagogue, JCC, *havurah*, school, camp, or other group or building, we hope the name we have selected will embody dreams and ideals for which we strive.

וּשְׁמְךָ עָלֵינוּ נִקְרָא

V'shimkha aleinu nikra

With all Your name on us
we will be called

Meditation

May the name we have chosen be associated with Torah, compassion, and deeds of righteousness. As our community journeys forward, may we be brought safely through the challenges of each stage of our growth and development.

Ritual

Print, carve, or embroider the name you have chosen onto a plaque, on a wall hanging, or in a community book, and have all who are witnesses to the new name and the dreams and ideals it evokes sign their names. When new members join your community, invite them to add their own names.

Blessing

(When the community has gathered to hear the new name given)

May we be known throughout Israel as

_____.

May this name become a blessed name.

May this place become a place of greatness.

May the One who blessed our ancestors bless all those
    who come to support this community today.

Teaching

And the Lord God formed out of the earth all the
wild beasts and all the birds of the sky, and brought
them to Adam to see what the human would call
them; and whatever the human called each living
creature, that would be his name.

(Genesis 2:19)

And you should take two onyx stones and carve
onto them the names of the children of Israel.

(Exodus 28:9)

I S R A E L

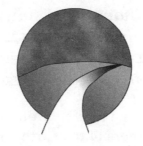

GOING TO ISRAEL

You have arrived early enough at the airport to check in for your flight to Israel. You know the routine: The ticket agents ask you for a photo ID, the security agents ask you questions to ensure your safety. But what if you were to hear their questions in a slightly different frame of mind?

והביאנו לשלום
מארבע כנפות הארץ,
ותוליכנו קוממיות
לארצנו

*Va'havi'einu l'shalom
mei'arba kanfot
ha'aretz, v'tolikheinu
kom'mi'yut l'artzeinu*

Bring us safely from the corners of the earth, and lead us in dignity to our holy land

Meditation

What is your name? (What is the meaning of the name by which you are called up to the Torah for an *aliyah*?)

What is the purpose of your trip to Israel? (What difference do you hope this trip might make?)

Did anyone help you pack? (Who has influenced you to take this trip? Who has readied your soul so that this will be a journey like no other?)

Did anyone give you anything to take with you?
(What experiences and what people symbolically accompany you?)

Did anyone speak with you before your trip? (What ancient words are spoken in the back of your mind as you depart?)

Ritual

As you wait to board your plane or during your flight, jot down answers to some of these questions. Tuck your answers into your passport so you can reflect upon them when you return. When your passport is stamped in Israel, see that image as a sign of a covenant between Israel and you.

Blessing
(As you board the plane)

יהי רצון...שתוליכנו לשלום...
ותגיענו למחוז חפצנו לחיים ולשמחה ולשלום.

Ye'hi ratzon...she'tolikhei'nu l'shalom...v'tagi'einu limchoz cheftzeinu l'chaim u'l'simchah u'l'shalom.

May it be Your will to lead us on the way of peace to our holy land, so that You will bring us happily to our destination, safe and sound.

(Tefilat Haderekh)

Teaching

There were several reasons for Rabbi Nachman's
voyage to the Land of Israel.... Indeed, for all the
things he did he never had a single reason, but
rather thousands and tens of thousands of deep
and elevated motivations—most especially so for
this great journey to *Eretz Yisrael*.

(*Rabbi Nathan, biographer of Rabbi Nachman
of Bratslav*)

Rabbi Nachman told Rabbi Yudil that he wanted
to go to the Land of Israel. Rabbi Yudil offered him
this blessing: "Great Rabbi! Surely you want to
perform some great things there. May it be God's
will to help you do that which you intend."

(Hayyeh Moharan)

VISITING JERUSALEM

I want to tell you a story that happened millennia ago. As thousands of Jews wound their way up to Jerusalem on *aliyat haregel*, pilgrimages, they were greeted along the way by people selling food and supplies and making music. As you go up to Jerusalem, imagine: What did they see? How did those pilgrims feel as they made their sacred journey? What did they anticipate? Imagine their awe as they saw the walls of Jerusalem for the first time, imagine how the stories they had heard as children now came alive.

כי מציון תצא תורה
ודבר ה' מירושלים

Ki mi'tzion tei'tzei Torah, u'dvar Adonai mi'Yerushalayim

The Torah shall emerge from Zion and God's word from Jerusalem

Meditation

As you travel through Jerusalem, continually ask yourself, how can I be a partner in realizing the Jerusalem for which I pray?

Ritual

For two thousand years, when it was impossible to ascend to Jerusalem except in our prayers, we could ascend only with our inner eye, as if it were a dream. Now we can ascend again, our feet touching the ground. What we see with our eyes, this miracle, is real.

ברוך אתה בונה ירושלים.

Barukh atah bonei Yerushalayim.

Blessed are You, Builder of Jerusalem.

The creator of this blessing never imagined a Jerusalem that would be so built up! We, too, never imagined a Jerusalem like the one before us. What happens when the reality before us exceeds the *brakhah*? We need a new *brakhah* that expresses our hopes that Jerusalem will continue to be built for many holy purposes: for peace, diversity, care, creativity, and a home for Torah.

As you look upon the lights of Jerusalem on the first night of your visit, close your eyes, just as you do when you light the Sabbath candles. Allow yourself to experience the transcendent power of your pilgrimage.

Blessing

ברוך אתה בונה ירושלים ל...

Barukh atah bonei Yerushalayim l'...

Blessed is the One who builds Jerusalem so that...

(To what end do you pray that Jerusalem will continue to be built? So that it will be a city of peace? So that it will be a model of pluralism? So that it will be a society based on *tzedakah* and *mishpat*—justice?)

Open your eyes and see that blessing fulfilled with your inner eye.

Teaching

תבנה חומות ירושלים.

Tivneh chomot Yerushalayim.

Rebuild the walls of Jerusalem.

(Psalms 51:20)

A reaching-up song: When God returned us to Zion
from exile, we thought we were dreaming.

(Shir Ha'ma'alot, *translated by Rachel Adler*)

They gathered throughout the towns and early in
the morning, the leader proclaimed: "Arise and let
us go up unto Zion." The flutes played before them;
governors, chiefs, and treasurers went out to meet
them. All the artisans in Jerusalem greeted them,
and the pilgrims would stand before the priest
with their gifts and tell the story: "My father was
a wandering Aramean who went down to Egypt...
and returned."

(Excerpts from Mishnah Bikurim *3:1–6)*

SENDING YOUR CHILD TO ISRAEL

Tonight I will take my son and daughter, who are going to Israel, to the airport. When my grandparents were alive, they gave us dollar bills to take to Israel and give to charity on our safe arrival. This was their prayer, their hope: that the *shliach mitzvah*, the one who performs a *mitzvah* on another's behalf, is guaranteed divine protection.

I summon the matriarchs and patriarchs as I give my own son and daughter dollar bills, and I say to them, "*Lekhi lakh*...Go to the land, for you are a blessing and shall be a blessing to others."

לֶךְ לְךָ ... לְכִי לָךְ...

Lekh l'kha...lekhi lakh...

Go to the land, and you shall be a blessing

Meditation

I will miss you. I am sending a part of myself with you. May your experience in Israel be intensely wonderful, intensely Jewish.

Ritual

Designate your child as your *shliach mitzvah* by giving him or her several dollar bills and this instruction: "When you arrive in Israel, seek out those who need *tzedakah*, and give them this money for me."

Blessing

You are a *shliach mitzvah,* an emissary of *mitzvot,* worthy of being showered with endless blessings.

יברכך ה' וישמרך.

Y'varekhekha Adonai v'yishm'rekha.

May God bless you and protect you.

Teaching

Go forth from your native land and from your parents' house to the land I will show you.

(Genesis 12:1)

A *mitzvah* protects and rescues while one is engaged in it.

(Babylonian Talmud: Sotah 21a)

RETURNING FROM ISRAEL

Just as you can choose to hear the questions the ticket and security agents have asked you as spiritual questions upon your departure, you can also choose to hear the questions the customs agents ask you upon your return as spiritual questions.

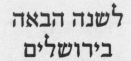

לשנה הבאה
בירושלים

*L'shanah ha'ba'ah
bi'Yerushalayim*

Next year in Jerusalem

Meditation

What did you bring back with you? (What relationships, memories, images, stories, promises, and commitments do you bring back?) What is its value? What souvenirs will you keep for yourself? What souvenirs are for others?

Ritual

When you get your photographs developed, arrange them in an album, giving each image a label of its own. Narrate your story, so you will never forget the meaning of each part of your visit.

Blessing

ברוך אתה הגומל לחיבים טובות.

Barukh atah ha'gomel l'chayavim tovot.

You have blessed me with this trip to Israel. I have been so moved, so touched. May I never forget the feeling I have right now for as long as I live.

Teaching

If I forget you, Jerusalem, let my strong hand wither.
If I do not remember you, let my tongue cleave to
the roof of my mouth, if I prefer not Jerusalem
above my chief joy.

(Psalms 137:5–6)

לשנה הבאה בירושלים.

L'shanah ha'ba'ah bi'Yerushalayim.

Next year in Jerusalem.

(Passover Haggadah)

TZEDAKAH

PREPARING OURSELVES TO DO SACRED WORK

Just as our sages raised their consciousness before engaging in sacred acts, we too can prepare ourselves for those everyday activities which we seek to elevate, as we discover how we can accomplish a sacred purpose—*avodah*—in all that we do.

הנני מוכן

Hin'ni mukhan

I am prepared

Meditation

Preparation, we learn, is what indicates that we want to make what we are about to do stand out. A *kavanah* is a meditative pause, an act of centering that allows us "to be fully present and aware of our place, our time…to feel God's presence."

הנני מוכן ומזמן.

Hin'ni mukhan u'm'zuman.

I am here, ready, prepared.

Ritual

Before you set out to do sacred work, pause and compose your own brief *kavanah* that names the sacred work you are about to do and reflects the kind of intention you hope to keep in mind.

For instance, if you are about to drop off cans of food at the neighborhood food pantry or soup kitchen, you might create a *kavanah* such as this: "Source of Blessing, allow me to find small and large ways that I can make a difference in people's lives."

Or, if you are about to perform a medical procedure on a patient or seek treatment for yourself, your *kavanah* might be, "Creator of the World, help and guide me to marvel in the wonder of the human body and to do all I can to sustain life."

Blessing

Here are some ways you might begin a *kavanah* that prepares you to do the sacred work of your life:

מקור הברכות

Mekor habrakhot _____ .

Source of Blessing, allow me to _____ .

בורא העולם

Borei ha'olam _____ .

Creator of the World, help and guide me to _____
_____ .

רבונו של עולם

Ribbono shel olam _____ .

Master of the Universe, make me aware of
_____ .

(As you conclude your *kavanah*)

תן בלבי להבין להשכיל לשמוע ללמוד וללמד.

Tein b'libi l'havin u'l'haskil lishmo'a lilmod u'l'lameid.

Allow my heart to understand, to enlighten, to listen, to learn, and to teach.

Blessed are You, God, who allows us to be fully present.

Teaching

All depends on the *kavanah* of the heart.

(Babylonian Talmud: Megillah 20a)

And Jacob awoke from his sleep and he said, "Surely God is in this place and I, I did not know."

(Genesis 28:16)

"And to serve God *(avodah)*" (Deuteronomy 11:13): This refers here to study. Just as serving at the altar is called *avodah*, so is study called *avodah*. Another interpretation of *avodah* refers to prayer. You might say, "Does this not refer to Temple *avodah*?" The answer is no, since Scripture says, "*Avodah*, do with all your heart and with all your soul" (Deuteronomy 11:13). Is there such a thing as Temple *avodah* in one's heart? Therefore, *avodah* refers to prayer. Just as service of the altar is called *avodah*, so is prayer called *avodah*.

(Sifre Deuteronomy, Piska *41*)

DONATING FOOD AND CLOTHING

In countless folktales, Elijah the prophet, a symbol of redemption, appears at our doorways as a poor, hungry wanderer. We invite him in, let him warm up by the fire, give him some food to sat- isfy his hunger and a coat to keep him warm. Redemption, we learn from these stories, happens in the most basic act of lovingkindness, sharing food and clothing with those in need.

ובחרת בחיים

U'vacharta ba'chaim

Make life-giving choices

Meditation

May the things we donate help to repair the world.

Ritual

As you gather together the things you will donate, ask yourself: If you were someone in need, which food or clothes would you be happy to receive? Supplement the clothes you plan to donate with a bag of new underwear or socks. If possible, call the local food pantry and ask what items are in short supply. Finally, make a swift delivery your priority.

Blessing

May the Merciful One continue to bless me and my family, and all that we have, just as our fathers and mothers were blessed. May we remember to thank You for sustaining us. May Your helping hand, which is open and overflowing, continue to be the source of blessing for us and all humanity.

Teaching

And Boaz said: Let her [Ruth] glean even among the best sheaves, and do not shame her.

(Ruth 2:16)

The Lord loves the righteous, the Lord watches over the stranger, giving courage to the orphan and widow.

(Psalms 146:8–9)

You are not required to complete the task, yet you are not free to evade it.

(Pirkei Avot 2:21)

Run to perform *mitzvot*…for one *mitzvah* leads to another *mitzvah*…and the consequence of a *mitzvah* is another *mitzvah!*

(Pirkei Avot 4:2)

SOLICITING SUPPORT

The root of the word that we often use to mean charity—*tzedakah*—is *tzedek*. *Tzedek* connotes justice and righteousness. Each time we do something that brings greater *tzedek* into the world, we are fulfilling the *mitzvah* of *tzedakah* and we become a partner for goodness. When we seek ever greater *tzedek* by soliciting support for a very good cause, we are inviting others to join us as partners in repairing this world.

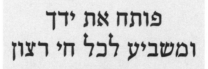

פותח את ידך
ומשביע לכל חי רצון

*Potei'ach et yadekha
u'masbi'a l'khol chai
ratzon*

Your open hand
sustains life

Meditation

May we know Your presence when we work together to repair the world.

הראיני מקבל/מקבלת עלי מצות הבורא:
ואהבת לרעך כמוך.

*Hareini (male:) m'kabel (female:) m'kabelet alai
mitzvat haborei: v'ahavta l'rei'akha kamokha.*

I hereby accept the obligation of fulfilling my Creator's
mitzvah: Love your neighbor as yourself.

Ritual

Before you pick up the phone, knock on the door, or compose your letter, pause to prepare yourself.

Remember: You are not doing this work alone. You are a partner of God, and you are about to encounter someone who is an image of God.

Think about God and Moses, together at the burning bush. They were both tense: God, to ask that a commitment be made, and Moses, to be asked to make such an awesome commitment. Remind yourself that at "burning bush moments," we need the courage to surmount our fears.

Blessing

(Before soliciting support)

Blessed is the Source of Life who elevates us to sacredness and bids us to immerse ourselves fully in the activities of Torah.

ברוך אתה גומל חסדים טובים לעמו ישראל.

Barukh atah gomel chasadim tovim l'amo Yisrael.

Blessed are You who fills us with goodness and leads us to acts of goodness.

Teaching

"Now the cry of the Israelites has reached Me; moreover, I have seen how the Egyptians oppress them. Come, therefore I will send you to Pharaoh, and you shall free My people, the Israelites, from Egypt." But Moses said to God, "Who am I that I should go to Pharaoh and free the Israelites from

Egypt?" And God said, "I will be with you; that shall be your sign that it was I who sent you. And when you have freed the people from Egypt, you shall worship God at this mountain."

(Exodus 3:9–12)

Tell the people of Israel to bring Me gifts; you shall accept gifts for Me from every person whose heart is so moved.

(Exodus 25:2)

And everyone who excelled in ability and everyone whose spirit moved him came, bringing...his offering...and all the wise women spun with their own hands and brought what they had spun....

(Exodus 35:25)

RECEIVING REQUESTS FOR CONTRIBUTIONS

The request comes by phone or through the mail. Yet another worthy cause is making its appeal: "We need your help now!" you are told. Each request comes from an organization that is making a real contribution, but the calls and letters are endless. Unable to take the time to examine the merits of each request, you feel hassled and overwhelmed, so it is easy to avoid the requests. However, you could choose to see this same scenario in a new way. What if you recognized that the calls and letters are coming your way because you have been generous enough to give before? What if you took pleasure in knowing that you are considered to be someone who cares?

נדיבות

Nedivut

Generosity

Meditation

Help me to realize that the people who call or write me are doing a *mitzvah*. They are doing the work of the *gabba'ei tzedakah*, the traditional *tzedakah* collectors, and I am privileged to honor them for their commitment. Help me to be patient with them and supportive of their efforts, even if I do not choose to make a contribution. Grant me the wisdom to know which causes I should be supporting this year and when I should be especially generous.

Ritual

Hold a family meeting so you can decide which causes are important to some or all of you and to which you will contribute. Let each member of the family have some say in making these decisions. Keeping in mind how difficult it can be to find presents each year for

family members, friends, and teachers, consider giving
the present of a donation (or a membership) in someone's honor, matching up the cause with the recipient
who will be touched by your gesture, made in his or
her name.

Blessing

(As you sit down together to make your decisions)

Blessed is the One who commands us to repair the world.

Teaching

The verse "They who provide charity for the many
are like stars forever and ever" (Daniel 12:3) refers
to collectors for charity.

(*Babylonian Talmud:* Baba Batra *8b*)

Rabbi Eleazar said: One who leads others to do
good is greater than one who oneself does good, for
it is said, "One who causes the giving of charity
confers peace" (Isaiah 32:17).

(*Babylonian Talmud:* Baba Batra *9a*)

Generosity does not begin with a lot of cash, but
with that wealth of spirit that shows others we care.
We esteem those who give with *nedivut* (generosity),
as did the biblical poet who said, "He who gives
freely to the poor, his beneficence lasts and lasts,
and his strength is exalted in honor" (Psalms 112:9).

(*Eugene Borowitz and Frances Weinman Schwartz,* The Jewish
Moral Virtues)

MAKING A CONTRIBUTION

Writing a check on behalf of a Jewish cause is a profound act of Jewish identity, a way we do our part in keeping the covenant. The checks we write for Jewish causes fulfill the *mitzvah* of *tzedakah*, sharing with others the fruits of our blessings and hard work. Our contributions will enable others to achieve survival, health, dignity,

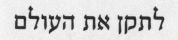

לתקן את העולם

L'takein et ha'olam

To repair the world

and fulfillment—the qualities implied when we speak of *tzelem elohim*, the idea that we are all made in the image of God. In the aftermath of a century that has placed so little value on human life, writing a check on behalf of a Jewish cause is witness to the value of human life in a concrete way.

Meditation

May these charitable endeavors and all those who offer help and support be blessed.

Ritual

As you file the receipts from charitable organizations for tax purposes, keep an added file of notes explaining why you chose these particular recipients for your *tzedakah* and how you hope the recipients will reach their goals. Don't hesitate to attach a copy of your "hopes" when you send in your check.

Blessing

(Before you write your check for *tzedakah*)

ברוך עוזר ומושיע ומגן.

Barukh ozer u'moshia u'magein.

Blessed is the One who helps, saves, and shields.

Teaching

Rabbi Eleazar would first give a coin to a poor person, and then pray, explaining: It is said, "Through charity I shall behold Your face."

(Babylonian Talmud: Baba Batra *10a)*

The focus on philanthropy, the creation of a society, and the restoration of the dignity of Jewish life have been the profoundest religious responses of the Jewish community to the Holocaust. The Nazis said, "Jewish life is not worth one-half a cent to put it out of its misery." Somebody else came along and said, "Have you anything to say that contradicts the Nazi testimony, other than the cheap and easy way of saying a prayer?" And one Jew, and another and then another said, "I say a Jewish life is worth a million dollars!" That became the power and testimony of UJA and Israel!

*(Irving [Yitz] Greenberg, "The Third Great Cycle
of Jewish History")*

DEDICATING A WALL OR PLAQUE THAT HONORS DONORS

The first time that our people proudly engraved their family names onto a public display was when they journeyed out of Egypt and into the desert. On precious stones, an artisan wrote each family name and placed them on the breastplate of the *kohein gadol*, the high priest. Wearing

ואלה שמות

V'eileh shmot

And these are the names

these names, the *kohein gadol* entered the inner chamber of the *mishkan*, the sacred tent, and chanted: "May it be a time of good will, of blessing, of abundance, of a rich harvest. May no one be shamed and may no one in Israel show mastery over another person."

Meditation

When we link our own family names to institutions or programs, we do so in the generous spirit of our ancestors.

Standing before these names, and summoning the memory of our loved ones, we affirm our commitments, encourage others to join us, and honor the deeds of the living. Reading these names, may our children and our children's children be reminded of our dedication to *tzedakah*, charitable giving, and *avodah*, holy work.

Ritual

After the wall or plaque is unveiled, join together in blessing to mark this occasion.

Then read aloud the names you are honoring, beginning with these words that introduce the Book of Exodus: *V'eileh shmot b'nei Yisrael*—And these are the names of the children of Israel: _____ .

Blessing

(After unveiling the wall or plaque, all say)

ברוך אתה ה׳ אלקינו מלך העולם
שהחיינו וקימנו והגיענו לזמן הזה.

*Barukh atah Adonai eloheinu melekh ha'olam
shehecheyanu v'kiy'manu v'higi'anu lazman hazeh.*

Blessed are You who has kept us in life, sustained us, and enabled us to reach this season.

Teaching

You shall make the breastplate thoughtfully.... The stones should correspond in number to the names of the sons of Israel: twelve, corresponding to their names. They shall be engraved like seals, each with its name, for the twelve tribes.

(*Exodus 28:15, 21*)

There are three crowns: the crown of the law, the crown of priesthood, and the crown of kingship. But the crown of a good name, to which anyone can aspire, is superior to them all.

(*Pirkei Avot 4:17*)

In my grandfather's memory, my aunt, who lived
with him, made a donation on behalf of our whole
family to a little Lubavitch *shul* in which he prayed.
A simple plaque was made. Hanging in the women's
section, it recalled my grandfather's kindness and
devotion to Judaism. When I visited my aunt and
prayed with her, we would sit right under the
plaque. I was always reminded of my grandfather's
tolerance for all the ways Judaism was expressed
by his family. I felt that he was there with us.

(*CLAL Faculty*)

WEARING YOUR COMMITMENTS

The Lion of Judah pin, Rabbi Irwin Kula teaches, "succeeded because it symbolically marks our identity and distinguishes us. Ritual uncovers the deeper meanings behind things. It is not that the pin itself is holy, but rather what the pin comes to mean *symbolically*—be it other people, one's past, one's responsibilities, and, for some, a sense of connection to something much bigger than themselves, a vision of humanity.... My experience is that the pin speaks from a much deeper place towards the healing of the world." When we put on any sign of our deep commitments, we are not just wearing jewelry or clothes: we are making a powerful declaration.

עוטר ישראל
בתפארה

Oteir Yisrael b'tifarah

You crown Israel with beauty

Meditation

May I meet the challenge of experiencing my full humanity, being observant enough to unveil the many sacred meanings in every object and in everything I do.

Ritual

When you put on a sign of your deep commitments, such as a Lion of Judah pin, be reminded that you inspire others to follow the example of caring that you set. When your children see you reciting a blessing over your sign and they ask you, "What makes this pin different from all other pieces of jewelry?" tell them, "It reminds me that I love all Jews, care for them, and use my resources to help Jews everywhere."

Blessing

(Before putting on your Lion of Judah pin or other sign of your
deep commitments)

ברוך אתה ה׳ אלקינו מלך העולם עוטר
ישראל בתפארה.

*Barukh atah Adonai eloheinu melekh ha'olam oteir
Yisrael b'tifarah.*

Blessed are You, Eternal One, our God, Sovereign of the World,
who crowns our people Israel with beauty.

(When you wear your Lion of Judah pin or other sign for
the first time)

ברוך אתה ה׳ אלקינו מלך העולם
שהחינו וקימנו והגיענו לזמן הזה.

*Barukh atah Adonai eloheinu melekh ha'olam
shehecheyanu v'kiy'manu v'higi'anu lazman hazeh.*

Blessed are You who has kept us in life, sustained us, and enabled
us to reach this season.

Teaching

How did Israel's journeying in the wilderness
proceed?… the trumpets sounded and Judah, led
by his standard, set out… Judah's stone being
turquoise, the color of his standard was something
like that of sky; embroidered on it was a lion.

(Numbers Rabbah 2:7)

We do boast about what we have financially with everything we own, do, or wear.... No one seems to find that offensive. How much more meaningful it is to wear a symbol that says, "Yes, I am blessed with financial well-being and security and I choose to share that blessing with my Jewish family wherever they may live and whenever they may need help from a world Jewish community that has not forgotten them. I am proud to wear a symbol that defines me and my values much more accurately than an expensive bauble."

(Helene Berger)

HOLY DAYS
Shabbat

LIGHTING SHABBAT CANDLES

It was through the light of the Shabbat candles that my grandmother would speak to God. With her fingers placed before her eyes, she would whisper a weekly update of the household and express the needs of her family members, one by one. Hers was the most direct prayer I have ever witnessed. "*Barukh Hashem, Barukh Hashem, Barukh Hashem,*" "Blessed is the Name," she would repeat three times. She'd wave her hands over the candles, then say the blessing, and Shabbat would slowly descend on the house.

להדליק נר

L'hadlik ner

Lighting the candles

Meditation

May the light of these candles bring joy, peace, and rest into this home.

Ritual

Place your Shabbat candles in the room in which you will be having dinner. As you light them, stand before your candles, letting your deepest, most personal prayers surface.

Blessing

ברוך אתה ה' אלקינו מלך העולם
אשר קדשנו במצותיו וצונו להדליק נר של שבת.

Barukh atah Adonai eloheinu melekh ha'olam asher kidshanu b'mitzvotav v'tzivanu l'hadlik ner shel Shabbat.

Blessed are You, Lord our God, whose *mitzvot* make our lives holy and who instructed us to light the Shabbat candles.

Teaching

Shabbat is a queen whose arrival changes the
humblest of homes into a palace.

(Adapted from Babylonian Talmud: Shabbat *119a)*

Through the extra soul given on Shabbat all
anxieties and irritations are forgotten, and only
joy rules.

(Zohar *II:204a*)

Why are we told to observe and remember
Shabbat? To learn that on the high seas or in the
desert, where you cannot observe Shabbat entirely,
you should remember it as much as you are able.

(Adapted from Pesikta Rabbati *23:1)*

I hear mother in her benedictions mention now one
name, now another. She names father, the children,
her own father and mother. Now my name too
has fallen into the flame of the candles. My throat
becomes hot. "May the Highest One give them his
blessing!" concludes mother, dropping her hands at
last. "Amen," I say.

(Bella Chagall, Burning Lights)

BLESSING CHILDREN ON SHABBAT

Our children keep changing, growing from dependent and delicious newborns to adventurous youngsters, to rebellious yet loving teenagers, to marvelous and complicated young adults. Our relationship to them keeps changing, too, but our wishes for them always stay the same. We want them to be blessed with

יברכך ה' וישמרך

Y'varekhekha Adonai v'yishm'rekha

May God bless you and protect you

health and happiness; we want them to know how much they are loved. In our hearts we wish the very best for our children every moment of every day. An ancient Jewish practice of setting aside a special time each week on Shabbat to bless our children encourages us to express our wishes for them aloud.

Meditation

May I have the wisdom to know what blessing my child truly needs.

May my child be able to receive my blessing and to know my love is deep and unconditional.

Ritual

Choose a special time each week, such as Friday night, at the start of the Sabbath, to give each child a personal blessing. You may want to use the ancient words, or you may want to combine them with your own words that express just what you feel. In Jewish tradition, parents place their hands on their children's heads as they bless them, but hugs also work, and so do just plain words. If you're away from your children at your regular blessing time, you can still "keep the appointment" by phoning or e-mailing during the day. One father even photocopies his hands and faxes them!

Blessing
(For sons)

ישמך אלקים כאפרים וכמנשה.

Y'simkha elohim k'Efraim v'kh'Menasheh.

May God make you like Ephraim and Menasheh.

(For daughters)

ישמך אלקים כשרה רבקה רחל ולאה.

Y'simekh elohim k'Sarah, Rivkah, Rachel, v'Leah.

May God make you like Sarah, Rebecca, Rachel, and Leah.

(For sons and daughters)

May God bless you and protect you,
May God's presence shine on you,
May God reach out to you tenderly and give you peace.

(Silently, or in a whisper, offer your personal blessing
for this week.)

Teaching

Noticing Joseph's sons, Israel asked, "Who are these?" Joseph said to his father, "They are my sons, whom God has given me here." "Bring them to me," he said, "that I may bless them." Now Israel's eyes were dim with age; he could not see. So Joseph brought his sons close to him, and he kissed them and embraced them...[and he blessed them, saying,] "May the angel who redeemed me from all harm bless these lads; in them may my name be recalled."

(Genesis 48:8–10, 16)

I am sending you Elijah the prophet before the coming of the great and awesome Day of the Eternal. He will turn the hearts of the parents to their children and the hearts of the children to their parents....

(Malachi 3:23–24)

When my students come for Shabbat dinner, I explain that in Jewish tradition, one's student is like one's child. So, as I bless my own daughters, I bless them, "May God bless you and protect you all the days of your life."

(CLAL Faculty)

HOLY DAYS
Rosh Hashanah

CHANGING YOUR FATE FOR THE COMING YEAR

Our tradition teaches that we can have a direct and active role in changing our fate for the coming year. While our desire to change our lives is par-ticularly strong during the days between Rosh Hashanah and Yom Kippur, we can make important changes all year long.

ותשובה ותפילה
וצדקה מעבירין
את רוע הגזרה

*U't'shuvah u't'filah
u'tzedakah ma'avirin
et ro'a ha'g'zeirah*

Turning, prayer, and deeds
can change our fate

Meditation

Help me to take a good look at my life and give me the courage to make changes I want to make. Guide me on my journey as I strive to make good changes, in myself and in the world in which I live.

Ritual

Jewish tradition teaches that you can change your fate in several ways:

Tzedakah: Changing the world.

Use your resources and talents to create more justice in the world. Decide: What can you do this day… this week…this month…to make an immediate difference?

Tze'akah: Crying out.

You can cry out about all that's unfair in the world, but you can choose other equally effective actions, such as letters, petitions, social action, prayers of words, and prayers of tears. Strategize: How can you increase the possibility that your most pressing outcry is heard?

Shinui hu'sheim: Changing your identity.

You can alter some aspect of your identity, expanding beyond the way others define you in your relationships and in your work. Ask yourself: How could a small adjustment in the way you see yourself allow you to recognize your own personal dreams and aspirations?

Shinui ma'aseh: Changing what you do.

You can break some old, familiar patterns of behavior, such as the way you relate to family, friends, or colleagues. Decide: If you were to commit yourself to establishing a new pattern of behavior at home, at work, or in the community, how could you increase the possibility that it becomes habit?

Blessing

(As you meditate upon the change you will make)

May we all be remembered and recorded in the Book of Life, blessing, sustenance, and peace.

(High Holidays liturgy)

Teaching

Rabbi Isaac said: "Four things change a person's fate, namely *tzedakah*, crying out, changing one's name, and changing one's conduct…and some say: changing one's place."

(Babylonian Talmud: Rosh Hashanah *16b)*

Will you hear our regrets? Will you release us from being prisoners of habit? Will you accept our prayers…and tune in to our heart's intent?

(Adapted from the Kol Nidrei service)

Accordingly, throughout the entire year, one should always look at oneself as equally balanced between merit and sin, and the world as equally balanced between merit and sin. If one performs even one sin, one tips one's balance and that of the entire world to the side of guilt and brings destruction upon oneself. [On the other hand,] if one performs even one *mitzvah*, one tips one's balance and that of the entire world to the side of merit and brings deliverance and salvation to oneself and others. This is implied by [Proverbs 10:25]: "A righteous person is the foundation of the world"; that is, one who acted righteously tipped the balance of the entire world to merit and saved it.

(Maimonides, Hilchot Teshuvah *3)*

Because the world is a different place each moment I am alive, there is unlimited potential for change.

(Kerry M. Olitzky and Rachel Sabath, Preparing Your Heart for the High Holy Days)

PREPARING YOUR PRAYERS FOR THE HIGH HOLIDAYS

You are racing to catch the last flight out to an urgent destination; you manage to board just as they close the gate. *Ne'ilah*—the service at the close of Yom Kippur—can feel like that. Your High Holidays can also run by in a mad dash. At the last moments of Yom Kippur, as you stand before the opened ark, you may feel as if the gates of prayer will shut before you've expressed your deepest prayers. However, you can choose to approach the gates of prayer in a new way. It requires getting your prayers for the new year ready and deciding how you'll affirm your prayers with your life.

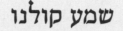

שמע קולנו

Shma koleinu

Hear our voice

Meditation

May I praise those with whom I live or work for the
blessing of who they are and what they do.

May I thank them for the specific ways they've
enriched and guided me.

May I ask them for precisely what I need now and in
the years to come.

May we forgive each other, initiating conversations
that clear the air.

May I put the prayers of my heart into action each day.

Ritual

Beginning on Rosh Hashanah and continuing each day before Yom Kippur, devote the time you need to discovering your own prayers. Let these four traditional kinds of prayer inspire you:

Hallel/ Praise: What wonders and miracles, both large and small, cause you to give praise this year?

Hoda'ot/ Thanks: What opportunities, relationships, gifts, ideas, even setbacks, make you thankful this year?

Bakashot/ Requests: What do you need real help in this year? Love, health, energy, stability, change, finding meaning?

S'lichot/ Forgiveness: What are you willing to pardon others for this year? What promises can you offer and make good on?

Practice your prayers, reviewing the ways you can affirm them with your life. If you wish, put your prayers and your commitments in writing to affirm them and bring them to synagogue during the High Holidays. Now, when you hear the final blast of the shofar, you'll be ready for a new year.

Blessing

(Whenever you have taken the time to prepare your prayers)

ברוך אתה הי שומע תפלה.

Barukh atah Adonai, shomei'a t'filah.

Blessed is the One who hears our prayers.

Teaching

Rabbi Eleazar said: Always prepare your prayer, rehearsing it, practicing it with your life. Then say it. Rabbi Abba said: Rabbi Eleazar's teaching is especially applicable to the prayers we say on Rosh Hashanah and Yom Kippur.

(Adapted from the Babylonian Talmud: Rosh Hashanah 35a)

What does it mean to live out your prayers with your life?

If your prayers are full of praise for the sun, moon, and stars, you would pay attention to the nighttime sky. You'd work to preserve the atmosphere, you'd study astronomy, celebrate the New Moon, and wear sunscreen.

If you are thankful for health, you would do your part to preserve or improve it. You would exercise, eat right, seek caregivers with the greatest wisdom. You would celebrate all the parts of your body that work well each day.

If your request is for peace, you would do your part to establish it in all the worlds you inhabit.

If your prayer is for forgiveness, you would resolve the lawn mower incident with your neighbor, you'd write a letter and forgive your senators for what they didn't do in the past year, and you would tell them what they must do now.

(CLAL Faculty)

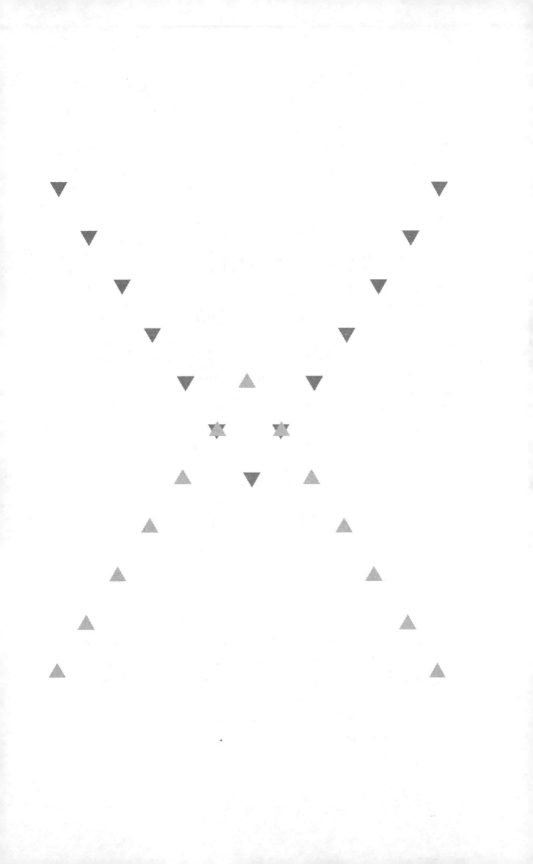

CASTING AWAY OUR SINS (*TASHLIKH*)

On Rosh Hashanah, I was walking my dog with a regular nighttime dog-walking companion who is not Jewish. He remarked: "Late this afternoon, as I was getting off the West Side Highway, I saw hundreds of people—I think they were Jewish—assembled by the edge of the Hudson River. They were throwing things into the river. What on earth were they doing?" How would I explain *tashlikh*, the ritual of throwing bread crumbs into a body of water, to my friend? "We are symbolically casting our sins away," I said, laughing to myself, imagining the sins of Manhattan cast off, floating toward Jersey. After the laughter, I began to think about the deeper meaning of the practice, the serious self-reflection that happens at the water's edge.

ותשליך במצולות ים
כל חטאתם

*V'tashlikh bimtzulot
yam kol chatotam*

You shall cast out our sins
into the depths of the sea

Meditation

On this Day of Judgment, I take account of my life and relationships during the last year. Of some things I am proud, of others disappointed or ashamed. I resolve to strengthen and sustain the many *mitzvot* I have performed—love in relationships, honesty in business, engagement in the repair of the world—and I resolve to cast off those actions or words that I regret. Help me to keep preserving what is good and to keep casting off what is bad. May this be a year of goodness and blessing.

Ritual

On the afternoon of the first day of Rosh Hashanah (the second day, if the first day falls on Shabbat), go to a body of water and cast away your sins symbolically by reaching into your pockets and throwing out "sins."

Blessing

(Before casting out your "sins")

May You cast out all the sins of Your people Israel into a place where they will not be remembered, nor counted, nor ever again be minded.

Blessed are You who enables me to distinguish between good and bad.

Teaching

You shall cast out our sins into the depths of the sea.

(Micah 7:19)

Yom Kippur atones only for transgressions between human beings and God. For transgressions between one individual and another, atonement is achieved only by reconciling with the person who has been offended.

(Mishnah Yoma 8:9)

When one forgets the essence of one's own soul, when one distracts one's mind from attending to the substantive content of one's own inner life, everything becomes confused and uncertain. The primary role of penitence, which at once sheds light on the darkened zone, is for one to return to oneself, to the root of one's soul. Then one will at once return to God, the Soul of all souls.

(*Avraham Isaac Kook,* The Lights of Penitence)

What should we be throwing into the water? Rabbi Richard Israel, of blessed memory, originated these tongue-in-cheek suggestions:

> For ordinary sins—white bread
>
> For exotic sins—French or Italian bread
>
> For dark sins—pumpernickel
>
> For complex sins—multigrain
>
> For truly warped sins—pretzels
>
> For sins of indecision—waffles
>
> For being ill-tempered—sourdough
>
> For excessive use of irony—rye bread
>
> For continual bad jokes—corn bread
>
> For hardening our heart—jelly doughnuts

HEARING THE SHOFAR

The sound of the shofar is primal. Part music, part siren, part animal cry, the blasts of the shofar focus our attention like nothing else. Adults crane their necks to see better; children are lifted onto shoulders to watch as the shofar is blown. Whole, broken, and whole again, the sounds shake us, awaken us, and stir us. Ultimately, they direct our attention to return to our hearts, our people, and our God.

תקיעה! שברים!
תרועה! תקיעה!

*T'kiah! Sh'varim!
T'ruah! T'kiah!*

The blasts of the shofar

Meditation

May each sound of the shofar awaken me to the sacred presence in all things.

Ritual

As you hear the shofar being blown, focus on the different sound combinations.

T'kiah! One blast: What does the first sound call you to remember?

Sh'varim! Three broken blasts: What felt broken in the past year?

T'ruah! Nine short broken notes: What does this alarm mean for your community?

T'kiah gedolah! The longest blast: What will you devote your breath and strength to in the coming year?

Allow all the sounds of the shofar to stir you, linking you to the past and the future, to individuals and community, to the place where you are now and to your commitments to the future.

Blessing

(Before the shofar is blown)

ברוך אתה ה' אלקינו מלך העולם
אשר קדשנו במצותיו וצונו לשמוע קול שופר.

*Barukh atah Adonai eloheinu melekh ha'olam asher
kidshanu b'mitzvotav v'tzivanu lishmo'a kol shofar.*

Blessed are You, Lord our God, who makes us holy with *mitzvot*
and gives us the *mitzvah* of hearing the sound of the shofar.

Teaching

Then you shall sound the horn loud; in the seventh
month, on the tenth day of the month—the day of
atonement—you shall have the horn sounded
throughout your land.

(Leviticus 25:9)

Shall the shofar be blown in the city and the people
not tremble?

(Amos 3:6)

Said Rabbi Abahu: Why do we sound the ram's
horn? The Holy One declared, "Sound the horn of a
ram before Me, that I may recall in your favor the
binding of Isaac, and consider you as having bound
yourselves, in faith, on the sacrificial altar."

(Babylonian Talmud: Rosh Hashanah 16a–b)

Blessed are the people who understand the shofar
sounds; they walk in God's light.

(Machzor)

HOLY DAYS
Yom Kippur

FASTING

Fasting may seem like a cruel test to see if we can deny our bodies food. Yet, at the heart of this practice is a desire to shift our attention away from the body's immediate needs and to focus on more spiritual concerns. The logic goes something like this: When we fast, we are faced with admitting our frailty. In that weakened state, we examine the parts of ourselves that are fragile and strengthen them with meditations and supplications. Fasting together as a community, we examine our failings and resolve to strengthen one another in the weeks to come.

הלא זה צום אבחרהו

Ha'lo zeh tzom evchareihu

This is the fast I choose

Meditation

When Rabbi Sheishet was fasting, he added these
  words to his daily prayers:
Master of the worlds:
We have learned that long ago,
in the days when the Temple still stood,
when people offered sacrifices as their atonement,
they offered only the fat and the blood.
That was sufficient to atone for them.
And now, when the Temple no longer stands,
I am fasting,
and, as a result, parts of me will be diminished.
Ye'hi ratzon,
May it be Your will:
To regard those parts of me that are diminished
as if I had offered them up before You upon an altar,
and may You show me favor.

(*Adapted from Babylonian Talmud:* Brakhot 17a)

Ritual

As you fast, move slower than usual, staying focused on the purpose of your fast.

Blessing

(As you begin your fast)

פותח את ידך ומשביע לכל חי רצון.

Potei'ach et yadekhah, u'masbia l'khol chai ratzon.

Open Your hand and fulfill each creature's needs.

Teaching

Why, when we fasted, did You not see?…This is My chosen fast: to loosen all the bonds that bind people unfairly, to let the oppressed go free, to break every yoke. Share your bread with the hungry, shelter the homeless, clothe the naked, and turn toward those in need. Then a cleansing light shall break forth like the dawn…then you shall call and the Lord will answer.

(Adapted from Isaiah 58)

And they fast on this day to approach a resemblance to the angels, inasmuch as the fast is consummated by humbling themselves, lowering their heads, standing, bending their knees, and singing hymns of praise. Then all the physical powers abandon their natural functions and engage in spiritual functions, as though having no animal nature.

(Judah HaLevi, The Kuzari *3:5, as quoted in S.Y. Agnon,* Days of Awe)

Penitence is inspired by the yearning of all existence to be better, purer, more vigorous and on a higher plane than it is. Within this yearning is a hidden life-force for overcoming every factor that limits and weakens existence. The particular penitence of the individual and certainly of the group draws its strength from this source of life, which is always active with never-ending vigor.

(*Abraham Isaac Kook,* The Lights of Penitence)

HOLY DAYS
Sukkot

BUILDING A *SUKKAH*

Each fall, our family would drag plywood and burlap out of the basement and build a *sukkah* in our backyard. We'd hammer on the sides, throw some pine branches on top, hang gourds from the roof, and carry down the kitchen table. It was our own makeshift harvest hut, a reminder of a stop on our way out of Egypt that our ancestors once took. In a family that spent much more time sitting inside and reading books than working outside with tools, Sukkot reconnected us to the natural world, and to the joy of both craft and creation.

לשב בסוכה

Leisheiv basukkah

Dwelling in the *sukkah*

Meditation

May this fragile *sukkah* remind us that in all things fragile, we find the presence of God.

Ritual

Build your *sukkah* from any materials you would like. You can use wood, pvc pipe, metal, or canvas. Here are the specifications: Your *sukkah* should have at least three walls, a natural see-through roof, and be able to accommodate at least one person seated comfortably. Invite family and friends to decorate with symbols of the Fall harvest, laminated Rosh Hashanah cards, and any other items that will enhance your celebration.

Blessing

(When you sit in your *sukkah*, say)

ברוך אתה ה' אלקינו מלך העולם
אשר קדשנו במצותיו וצונו לשב בסוכה.

*Barukh atah Adonai eloheinu melekh ha'olam asher
kidshanu b'mitzvotav v'tzivanu leisheiv ba'sukkah.*

Blessed is the Holy One who instructs us to dwell in the *sukkah*.

Teaching

You shall live in *sukkot* seven days; all citizens of
Israel shall live in *sukkot*, in order that future generations may know that I made the Israelite people
live in *sukkot* when I brought them out of the land
of Egypt.

(Leviticus 23:42–43)

I have singled out Bezalel…I have endowed him
with a divine spirit of skill, ability, and knowledge
of every craft…and I have also granted this art to
all who are skillful, so that they may make everything that I have instructed you.

(Exodus 31:1–3, 6)

RECEIVING *SUKKAH* GUESTS

Each Sukkot, we are visited by two sets of guests in our *sukkah*. The first guests are the family and friends that bundle up in sweaters, sip hot soup, and laugh at our cranberry and popcorn garlands. Our second guests are the ancient ones, called the *ushpizin*, the spirits whose life stories are woven into the Torah. It is said that the interaction of these two sets of guests makes eating in the *sukkah* so magical. The Divine Presence, lured down by the laughter and joyous prayer, hovers between the bamboo roof and the stars.

תיבו תיבו אושפיזין דמהימנותא, תיבו בצלא דקודשא בריך הוא

*Tivu tivu ushpizin
dimheim'nutah, tivu
b'tzi'la d'kudsha,
Brikh hu*

Be seated, be seated,
guests of faithfulness,
be seated in the shade
of the Holy One

Meditation

Be present among us, spreading over us a shelter of Your peace, and surrounding us with the pure light of Your holiness. And to those who hunger and thirst, bring bread and satisfying water. May we merit to live many days on the earth, on holy land, to do our work with reverence. Blessed is God forever, Amen and Amen.

(Ushpizin *blessing*)

Ritual

When inviting guests to your *sukkah*, let them know beforehand that you will each "invite" your own *ushpizin*, ancestors or mentors whose lives and teachings have had a special impact on you. Encourage guests to bring along pictures or mementos which will allow them to better recall their *ushpizin* and to tell their stories. Help your guests to welcome the *ushpizin* by saying, "Each one of us has received an important 'torah,' a teaching, from people dear to us. Just as the Torah has been transmitted by God to Moses to Joshua to the elders, and so on down, we have received maxims and examples of how to live and love from our familiar guides. In this way, our *ushpizin* have been rabbis—teachers—to us." As you invite your *ushpizin* into the *sukkah*, explain why they are special to you and share their teaching, beginning by saying: "I invite to our meal my exalted guest, Reb so-and-so. Reb so and so taught me...." (*Reb* is an endearing form of the word rabbi, expressing honor, love, and intimacy.) For example, Reb Sidney, my father-in-law, used to say that whenever he traveled, the sun shined. I think he meant that if you acted as if all was well in the world, you could feel better about whatever came your way.

Blessing

(As you are seated in the *sukkah*)

ברוך אתה ה' אלקינו מלך העולם
אשר קדשנו במצותיו וצונו לשב בסוכה.

*Barukh atah Adonai eloheinu melekh ha'olam asher
kidshanu b'mitzvotav v'tzivanu leisheiv ba'sukkah.*

Blessed are You, our God, who makes our lives sacred with *mitzvot*
and instructs us to dwell in the *sukkah*.

(As you invite your *ushpizin*)

תיבו תיבו אושפיזין צלאין,
תיבו תיבו אושפיזין קדישין,
תיבו תיבו אושפיזין דמהימנותא,
תיבו בצלא דקודשא בריך הוא.

*Tivu tivu ushpizin ela'in, tivu tivu ushpizin
kedishin, tivu tivu ushpizin dimheim'nutah,
tivu b'tzi'la d'kudsha, Brikh hu.*

Be seated, be seated, exalted guests; be seated, be seated, holy
guests; be seated, be seated, guests of faithfulness; be seated in the
shade of the Holy One.

Teaching

You shall live in *sukkot* for seven days; all of Israel shall live in *sukkot* to teach the future generations that the people of Israel lived in *sukkot* when I brought them out of the land of Egypt.

(Leviticus 23:42–43)

Moses received Torah from God at Sinai. He transmitted it to Joshua, Joshua to the elders, the elders to the prophets, the prophets to the members of the Great Assembly.

(Pirkei Avot *1:1*)

WAVING THE *LULAV* AND *ETROG*

Returning from the Lower East Side after having purchased my *lulav* (palm branch, myrtle, and willow) and *etrog* (citron) for Sukkot, I got on the subway and headed home. Other passengers in my car looked my way with wonder. After a few stops, one woman inquired about my strange "bouquet." I told her it was a symbol of the Fall harvest—peace, unity, and fertility—that I would use in my holiday celebration. "What do you do with it?" she asked. "We shake it in all directions," I said. "Do it right," she said, "it sounds important."

ושמחת בחגך

V'samachta b'chagekha

And you shall rejoice in your festival

Meditation

As I shake this symbol of life in the six directions, may You sustain life in each direction—across the seas, in the deserts, on mountain tops and ice caps, skyward to the clouds, deep down in the earth's soil, and to the cosmos, which frames them all.

Ritual

Standing with the *etrog* in your left hand, stem down, and the *lulav* in your right, place your hands together. After reciting the blessings, turn the *etrog* stem up, stretch out your arms and shake three times in each of the six directions (first to the east, then south, west, north, up, and down).

Blessing

(As you hold the *lulav* and *etrog* in your hands)

ברוך אתה ה׳ אלקינו מלך העולם
אשר קדשנו במצותי וצונו על נטילת לולב.

*Barukh atah Adonai eloheinu melekh ha'olam, asher
kidshanu b'mitzvotav v'tzivanu al netilat lulav.*

Blessed is the Holy One who makes us holy and instructs us to
raise up the *lulav*.

(When you make this blessing for the first time on Sukkot)

ברוך אתה ה׳ אלקינו מלך העולם
שהחינו וקימנו והגיענו לזמן הזה.

*Barukh atah Adonai eloheinu melekh ha'olam
shehecheyanu v'kiy'manu v'higi'anu lazman hazeh.*

Blessed are You who has kept us in life, sustained us, and enabled
us to reach this season.

Teaching

On the first day, you shall take the fruit of the *hadar* tree (an *etrog* or citron), branches of palm tree, and willows of the brook, and you shall rejoice before the Lord your God seven days.

(Leviticus 23:40)

Rejoicing by waving the palm branch, myrtle, willow, and citron may seem strange. Why these four species? Why wave plants at all? For our ancestors, these species were symbols of their basic needs. Each palm tree yielded more than a hundred pounds of dates, sugar and wine were made from the sap, and leaves were woven into baskets. The sweet smell of the citron was a perfume, the berries of the myrtle a seasonal treat, and the willows provided them with shade. Symbolically, rejoicing with the four species was, and still is, a deep expression of gratitude for having those things that sustain us.

(CLAL Faculty)

TAKING DOWN A *SUKKAH*

Our community really took shape as we built our *sukkah* together. During the holiday, we had deep bonding experiences as we left the private, protected shelters of our own homes and apartments and joined together in our communal *sukkah* to eat, laugh, and sing together under the stars that twinkled through the pine boughs. As the holiday was ending and the decorations were in tatters, we felt we needed to mark the last moments of being in our *sukkah*, and to say farewell to its shelter, its fragile beauty, and its promise. On the last afternoon of Sukkot, most of the folks who had built our *sukkah* gathered and we drank a toast to our little group. We promised ourselves that we would find ways to keep our fellowship alive those many weeks until Chanukah, when we would again celebrate another season of our lives.

הושיעה את עמך

Hoshiah et amekha

Bless us, sustain us

Meditation

Just as we have found beauty together as we have dwelled in this *sukkah*, may we find beauty together all year as we dwell in each other's lives.

Ritual

All who have built the *sukkah* together join once again to say farewell, with a toast and a blessing. At this last gathering, make concrete plans to keep your fellowship until the next holiday season.

Blessing

(As you contemplate how you can continue to bring the feeling of
being together, sheltered in the *sukkah*, all year round, you recite
for the last time this year)

We praise You, Eternal God, Ruler of the Universe, who has made
us holy with Your *mitzvot* and commanded us to fulfill the *mitzvah*
of dwelling in the *sukkah*.

הושיעה את עמך וברך את נחלתך.

Hoshiah et amekha u'varekh et nachala'tekhah.

Bless us and save us and our heritage; shelter
and sustain us forever.

Teaching

Our sages taught that at the end of days, God will
make a huge *sukkah* out of the skin of the Leviathan,
an enormous mythical beast, for all the righteous in
Jerusalem. In our own *sukkah*, at the end of the holiday, we said farewell to the *sukkah* in the traditional
way: "May it be Your will, Lord our God and the
God of our ancestors, that just as we have fulfilled
the *mitzvah* of dwelling in the *sukkah*, may we
deserve to dwell in the *sukkah* of the Leviathan next
year in Jerusalem." We imagined our little *sukkah*
suddenly becoming the silvery scale of a wonderful
sea monster, and we imagined all of us transported
to Jerusalem. Bidding farewell to our *sukkah*, we
imagined a world ready to greet the Messiah.

(CLAL Faculty)

HOLY DAYS
Simchat Torah

DANCING WITH THE TORAH

There is a tradition that if the Torah is dropped, all who are present must fast for forty days. In other words, the Torah makes for a difficult dance partner, particularly on Simchat Torah, when we hold onto the Torah with all our strength, as we whirl, twirl, and spin around. Dancing with the Torah is like dancing with your newborn children and your parents at the same time. We dress the Torah like a newborn and cradle it, kiss it, and protect it. We respect the Torah like a parent, challenge it, and learn from its words.

שמחת תורה

Simchat Torah

The joy of Torah

Meditation

I embrace this Torah in my arms, and the Torah embraces me. Together, we dance.

Ritual

Hold on to the Torah, placing one hand underneath it and on its handles, and the other around its waist. Lean it to your left side, over your heart. Then dance! There are no right or wrong steps, only steps of joy. Even standing still with the Torah in your arms is a "Torah dance"! When it is time to pass on the Torah scroll, seek someone who may not yet have had the opportunity to dance with the Torah—on this day, or ever in their lives.

Blessing

(As you are given a Torah scroll to hold, or as you enter into the circle of dancers)

Blessed is the Holy One who gives us the gift of Torah.

Teaching

And Miriam the prophet, the sister of Aaron, took
a tambourine in her hand, and all the women went
out after her with tambourines, and all the women
danced.

(Exodus 15:20)

Singers and dancers alike will say: "All my roots
are in You."

(Psalms 87:7)

Praise God's name in dance.

(Psalms 149:3)

And father, always so quiet, so calm, moves from
his place, makes his way toward the dancing men,
and falls into the whirling ring. The chain of people
gives a tug and swallows him.... From the corner
I watch father. I look for him among the dancers.
There is his head, slightly bent to one side, his
eyes lowered, his long beard afloat. There he is,
whirling as in a sweet dream, his whole body
melting with pleasure.

(Bella Chagall, Burning Lights)

Simchat Torah is intended to be crowded, so use
a space that is a bit too small...so that people can
crowd in and be intimate and close, and so the
music is loud and strong.

(Sarah Shendelman and Avram Davis, Traditions)

HOLY DAYS
Chanukah

LIGHTING THE MENORAH

Whereas Shabbat candles are meant to brighten the table, Chanukah candles are placed by the window. Why don't we display our Chanukah menorah on our table? One reason is *pirsum ha'nes*, to publicize the miracle of Chanukah, but another reason concerns the special nature of the lights themselves. The Chanukah lights are meant *solely* for enjoyment and celebration—they are *not* to be used for any practical task, like giving light or making a table more beautiful. We try not to look at them and say: "What other use can these lights be to me?" Perhaps this tradition can teach us this: to appreciate, joyously, things for just what they are.

הנרות הללו

Ha'neirot ha'lalu

We light these lights

Meditation

May these Chanukah lights guide us to appreciate people and things for what they are.

Ritual

Sing the Chanukah blessings first and then light your menorah.

Here's how it is done: Place one candle on the right of the menorah, adding one more candle each subsequent night. After lighting the *shames* (the candle used to light all the others), kindle the newest light first, moving from left to right.

Blessing

ברוך אתה ה׳ אלקינו מלך העולם
אשר קדשנו במצותיו וצונו להדליק נר של חנוכה.

*Barukh atah Adonai eloheinu melekh ha'olam asher
kidshanu b'mitzvotav v'tzivanu l'hadlik ner shel
Chanukah.*

Blessed is the Holy One who instructs us to light the
Chanukah candles.

ברוך אתה ה׳ אלקינו מלך העולם
שעשה נסים לאבותינו בימים ההם בזמן הזה.

*Barukh atah Adonai eloheinu melekh ha'olam she'asah
nisim la'avoteinu, bayamim ha'heim, bazman hazeh.*

Blessed is the Holy One who made miracles for our ancestors and
makes miracles for us.

(On the first night only, add)

ברוך אתה ה׳ אלקינו מלך העולם
שהחיינו וקימנו והגיענו לזמן הזה.

*Barukh atah Adonai eloheinu melekh ha'olam
shehecheyanu v'kiy'manu v'higi'anu lazman hazeh.*

Blessed are You who has kept us in life, sustained us, and enabled
us to reach this season.

Teaching

On the 25th of Kislev, we begin the eight days of
Chanukah.... For when the Greeks entered the
Temple, they defiled all the oils therein, and when
the Hasmonean dynasty prevailed against and
defeated them, they made a search and found only
one cruse of oil that lay with the seal of the high
priest but which contained sufficient oil for one
day's lighting only; yet a miracle was wrought and
they were able to light the lamp for eight days.

(Babylonian Talmud: Shabbat 21b)

During all eight days of Chanukah, these lights are
sacred, and we are not permitted to make any other
use of them aside from celebrating the miracle.

(Chanukah prayer)

The light of the menorah is not for working by, but
is a holy light to guide our souls.

(Sarah Shendelman and Avram Davis, Traditions)

REDEDICATING YOUR HOME ON CHANUKAH

After the Maccabees drove Antiochus's army out of the Holy Temple in Jerusalem, the Jews performed a ceremony to restore holiness to their sacred space. The ceremony was called *chanukat habayit*—literally, "rededicating the house." Our ancestors lit a menorah and, in its glow, they reclaimed their home. In our own time, at Chanukah, we think about our own homes as places where we encounter the sacred, deepening the way we experience home as a holy place.

מזמור שיר
חנוכת הבית

Mizmor shir chanukat ha'bayit

Sing out the melody that rededicates the house

Meditation

My home is the place where I celebrate life, mark the seasons, welcome guests, light candles, remember the past, dream about the future, and open my heart to the present. At Chanukah, may I rededicate my home to the values and relationships I hold sacred.

Ritual

Here are eight ways to rededicate your home:

1. Rededicate the rooms of your home so they can better accomplish their sacred tasks—the dining room for guests, the kitchen for sustaining life, the living room for family interaction, the bedroom for rest and intimacy.

2. Invite guests, cook a special meal together, plan a family event or make time for those you love, creating and expanding *shalom bayit*, relationships of peace.

3. Make your home a place where learning, *talmud Torah*, leads to change. Create or enlarge your shelf for Jewish books.

4. Read a Jewish book from a challenging perspective.

5. Choose a place in your home where you can devote yourself to contemplation and prayer. Make a *mizrach*—a marker pointing eastward—and put it up on your own eastern wall to focus your prayers toward Jerusalem.

6. Stand facing your *mizrach*, and experiment with different ways to direct your heart in *tefilah*, meditation.

7. As the Chanukah lights burn, gather coats and blankets in your home to deliver to a local shelter, or collect canned food for a food drive.

8. Place boxes for *tzedakah* in each room of your home so they will be available for collecting loose change.

Blessing

(As you prepare to perform each night's deed of rededication)

As this menorah fills with light, may our home be rededicated to the Source of Blessing that connects us all.

Teaching

And on the 25th day of Kislev...the sanctuary of
God was dedicated anew with song and music....
Then Judah and his brothers with all the people of
Israel ordained that the Days of the Dedication
of the altar should be celebrated from year to year
for eight days in gladness and thanksgiving.

(1 Maccabees 5)

There are seven dedications that have been
achieved by light: "The creation of the world by
moonlight, the Tabernacle and two Temples by
the seven-branched menorah, the festival of the
Maccabees by the eight-branched menorah,
the walls of Jerusalem by torches, and the
millennium by the sevenfold light of the sun."

(Pesikta Rabbati 2)

HOLY DAYS
Purim

PREPARING *MISHLOACH MANOT*

As a child, I remember going to synagogue on Purim dressed in a crazy costume to hear the *Megillah* reading, and I remember receiving *mishloach manot*, plates or baskets of treats from friends. What a perfect holiday for kids— we got to eat all sorts of cakes, candies, fruits, and, of course, *hamentashen*. As I got older, I began to realize how *mishloach manot* (some call it *shalach manos* in Yiddish) was taking on new meaning for me. It has become more important to me to give *mishloach manot* than to receive. It's about the joy of giving, the pleasure of making the packages, deciding on the right food for the right person, keeping in mind their food preferences or food allergies. It's like taking the time to find the perfect birthday gift for a friend, an effort that expresses our special connection.

חברים כל ישראל

Chaverim kol Yisrael

The fellowship of the entire people Israel

Meditation

May I prepare and give these gifts with a full and open heart. May we be blessed on Purim and on each day of our lives with light, gladness, and honor and with the gift to express our friendship.

Ritual

For Purim, prepare plates or baskets of *mishloach manot* for at least one friend. You'll want to include a variety of ready-to-eat foods, such as a fruit, a cake, nuts, or a bottle of juice or wine. Involve family members in planning, preparing, decorating, and delivering the *mishloach manot* to two friends, neighbors, and to people in hospitals or nursing homes. If many of the people you know are unfamiliar with this ritual, include a note explaining what it's all about and what it means to you. Let them know that one way to celebrate Purim is by celebrating our friendships with tasty gifts. Next Purim, don't be surprised to find *mishloach manot* baskets on your doorstep.

Blessing

(As you begin to prepare your *mishloach manot*)

Bless us and all people with joy, gladness, and friendship.

Teaching

The month which was turned unto them from sorrow to gladness, and from mourning into a good day; that they should make them days of feasting and gladness, and of sending portions to one another, and gifts to the poor.

(Megillat Esther 9:22)

No true Jewish *simcha* is complete unless it is shared with friends and with the needy.

(*Irving [Yitz] Greenberg*, The Jewish Way)

SENDING BASKETS

If we can only weave these fragile reeds
    together
The bulrushes will be a basket,
The papyrus will be parchment,
The days will be stories....

If we can take
what is random—our lot,
and make it our portion.

Then we will hold ourselves
as we were held at birth
in cradles and bassinets—
as things of light and joy,
as gifts.

(Tamar Stern)

HOLY DAYS
Passover

REMOVING *CHAMETZ* FROM ONE'S HOME

The tradition is ancient, the experience powerful. Starting as much as a week or more before Passover, the scrubbing, scouring, boiling, and burning begins. The cleaning includes a thorough check for *chametz* (non-Passover foods) in the pantry, fridge, freezer, and cupboards. Things like opened boxes of cereal and spaghetti are packed into boxes alongside the various other nonperishable products. When we have separated out all the leaven and have cleaned everything imaginable, from children's toys to book jackets, there is a final ritual of checking for leaven called *bedikat chametz*.

זמן חרותנו

Z'man cheiruteinu

The season of our freedom

Meditation

You bless us with the commandment to remove all *chametz* from our homes; may it be Your will that we find the way to remove the *chametz* of our souls, by finding and sharing freedom.

Ritual

The tradition of ridding the house of *chametz* includes a variety of practices. There are contracts for selling one's *chametz* to a non-Jew, candlelit searches for the last remaining leaven, and the burning of crumbs the morning before the seder.

There is another way you can remove *chametz* from your home. Take all foods in closed containers that are traditionally not eaten on Passover and bring them to the nearest food pantry or shelter. Find neighbors who might appreciate the remains of your open containers and refrigerated foods. Explain that you are about to celebrate the Festival of Freedom, and that this is part of your "soul preparation."

A third way to remove *chametz* is symbolic, according to the Hasidic masters. The *mitzvah* of *bedikat chametz* (inspecting for *chametz*) teaches that the work of liberation begins with careful attention to the hidden *"chametz"* in us and around us, symbolizing the oppression and slavery beneath our ordinary gaze. Each of us, in our own way, can remove those things that block our fullest freedom and the freedom of others.

Blessing

(After you have distributed the foods)

All leaven in my possession, whether I have seen it or not, whether I have removed it or not, is hereby nullified and ownerless as the dust of the earth. Blessed is God, Ruler of the Universe, who has commanded us to look carefully for *chametz* and to turn it into blessing for those around us.
You bless us with the commandment to remove all *chametz* from our homes; may it be Your will that we find the way to remove the *chametz* of our souls, finding freedom.

Teaching

Seven days you shall eat unleavened bread; on the very first day you shall remove leaven from your houses.

(Exodus 12:15)

In preparation for Passover, traditional Jews totally eliminate *chametz*—not just bread but any and all forms of leaven—from the house and the diet. This is a symbolic statement of cutting off from the old slave existence and entering the new condition of living as a free person. The decisive break with previous diet is the outward expression of the internal break with slavery and dependence. For the modern celebrant, it is a critical step in the process of liberation that finally leads to freedom.

(*Irving [Yitz] Greenberg,* The Jewish Way)

SEARCHING FOR THE *AFIKOMAN* (FOR GROWN-UPS)

Given the high-tech nature of entertainment now available to children, it is amazing that searching for the *afikoman* continues to be a source of anticipation, fun, and memory. We can build upon the popularity of this beloved Passover ritual, increasing awareness of our potential for greater spirituality, commitment to Judaism, and creative transformation of Jewish life by adding a new practice to our Passover seder. It's called "*afikoman* for grown-ups." This is a search for the themes of Passover that are already in our environments. We just need to notice them!

צפון

Tzafoon

Discovery of the hidden

Meditation

May I always keep searching for the hidden possibilities that are within my reach.

Ritual

Here's how to play "*afikoman* for grown-ups." At the seder, after the young people have searched for the *afikoman*, invite everyone (kids can play, too) to search for signs of Passover themes. Select any one of these themes: renewing life (*karpas*), being free (matzah), telling our sacred story (*maggid*), feeding the hungry (*ha lachma anya*), asking important questions (*mah nishtanah*), honoring multiple voices (*arba'ah banim*), connecting to past generations (*b'khol dor va'dor*), celebrating life (*hallel*), and yearning for sacred space (*l'shanah ha'ba'ah bi'Yerushalayim*). Get up from the seder table and search your home—or your host's home (getting permission first)—for all the different ways your Passover theme is reflected in people, places, and things. For instance, if "renewing life" is an important theme for you, look for signs of springtime, personal and spiritual growth, new interests, new family members, rekindled relationships, pruning back, getting second chances, planning for the future, renovation. If you've found daffodils, slipcovers, or a pregnant guest, you're on the right track.

Returning to the table, share the theme you've searched for and describe evidence you've found. The discoveries you've all made—the daffodils, the slipcovers—are symbols of sacred commitments, just like the *haroset*, matzah, and *maror*. If you have been a seder guest at someone else's home, search for signs of your Passover theme when you return to your own home.

Blessing

(After you've shared the theme you've chosen and described the evidence you've found)

Just as some keep a piece of the *afikoman* all year long as a sign of God's blessings, may the hidden *afikoman* I discover be a sign of God's blessings.

Teaching

In the end, we will find *afikoman*. We will find the hidden matzah, the hidden awareness, the hidden parts of the soul.

(Rabbi Nachman of Bratzlav)

Many commentators believe that the *afikoman* is reserved for the end of the meal so that matzah would be the last taste of the celebration. A striking commentary by Rabbi Harold Schulweis suggests that the *afikoman* is the matzah of the future (messianic) redemption. The matzah is broken because the world is still unredeemed; the matzah is eaten at the end because our hope is still unbroken.

(*Irving [Yitz] Greenberg*, The Jewish Way)

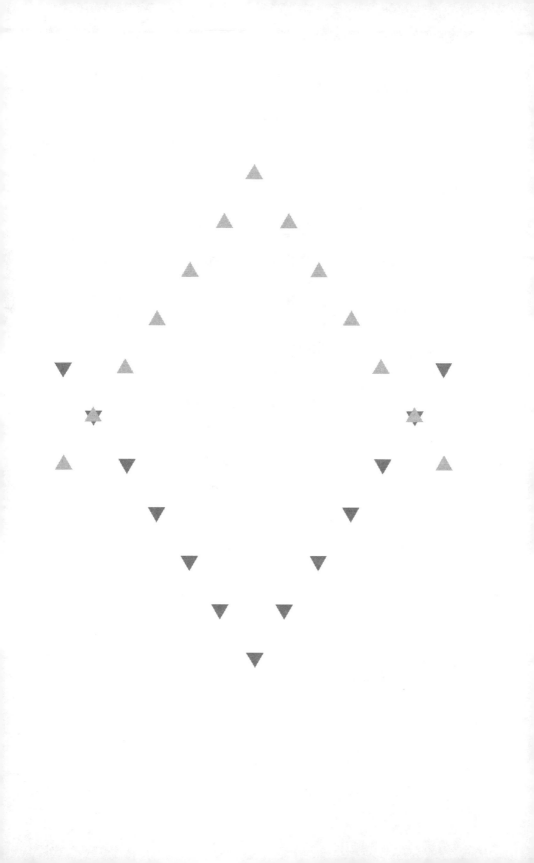

COUNTING THE *OMER*

The rhythms of our ancestors' lives were set by the agricultural cycles and the accompanying rituals performed for each season at the Temple in Jerusalem. *Sfirat Ha'omer*, the counting of the *omer*, was one of the most carefully observed of these rituals. The priests would offer a measure of harvested crop, or *omer*, on the second day of Passover. All of Israel would then begin counting the days between Passover and Shavuot, forty-nine days in all. Although we no longer have the Temple, we still count. Counting the days from the sea-crossing freedom of Passover to the Torah-receiving commitment of Shavuot—the "counting the *omer*"—guides us in reaffirming that each day we progress, clarify, and act with our ultimate goals in mind.

הנני מוכן ומזמן לקיים מצות עשה של ספירת העומר

Hin'ni mukhan u'm'zuman l'kayeim mitzvat asei shel sfirat ha'omer

I am ready to fulfill the *mitzvah* of counting the *omer*

Meditation

As I count each day between Passover and Shavuot, may I remain awake to the full potential and special texture of each passing moment. As I count *from* one moment *to* the next, may I be helped to act in light of that wakefulness, appreciating my freedom *from*, and my commitment *to*.

הנני מוכן ומזומן לקיים מצות עשה של ספירת העומר.

Hin'ni mukhan u'm'zuman l'kayeim mitzvat asei shel sfirat ha'omer.

I am ready to fulfill the *mitzvah* of counting the *omer*.

Ritual

Beginning on the second night of Passover, toward the end of the seder, recite the blessing for counting the *omer* and announce that day's count (remember, the Jewish "day" begins the evening before). On the forty-eight subsequent days, find an appropriate (and easily remembered!) moment to count that day's *omer*—as you kiss your children good night, or when you set out your clothes for the next day. Most Jewish calendars will have the day's count as a reminder. As you count each subsequent evening, focus on how you change as you move from awareness (Passover) to action (Shavuot).

Blessing

ברוך אתה ה׳ אלקינו מלך העולם
אשר קדשנו במצותיו וצונו על ספירת העומר.

Barukh atah Adonai eloheinu melekh ha'olam asher kidshanu b'mitzvotav v'tzivanu al sfirat ha'omer.

Blessed are You, Eternal God, Ruler of the Universe, whose *mitzvot* teach us holiness and who commands us to count the *omer*.

Teaching

You shall count from the eve of the second day of Passover, when an *omer* of grain is to be brought as an offering, seven complete weeks.

(Leviticus 23:15)

The *omer* is the amount of ground and sifted barley offered as a sacrifice. The *omer* is thus neither time, nor barley, but a measurement. Why do we count a measurement? In Exodus 16:16, we learn that when the Israelites were in the desert they each received lifegiving manna according to their need: one *omer* per person—no more, no less. Overzealous gatherers discovered that any manna in excess of an *omer* spoiled before it could be eaten. Fastidious gatherers, on the other hand, never came up short. An *omer* is thus the symbol of the precise amount to sustain someone. Maybe the period of the *omer* is for figuring out what we need to sustain us and how much. The days of the *omer* are not about counting time, but weighing an *omer*'s worth of what counts.

(Dan Judson, Sh'ma)

HOLY DAYS
Yom Ha'atzma'ut

CELEBRATING YOM HA'ATZMA'UT, ISRAEL'S INDEPENDENCE DAY

Each time we mark the birth of the State of Israel, we affirm our connection to the land and to the places that link us to our historical heritage. We celebrate how much Israel has accomplished in such a short time. We have established a home and a sanctuary; we have a flourishing Israeli culture, world-renowned hospitals and universities, success in agriculture, industry, and technology. On this day, we also take the opportunity to reflect on the dreams we hold for Israel. Doing so, we renew our commitment to keep reimagining an Israel that fulfills and goes beyond our dreams.

נודה לך על הארץ

Nodeh l'kha al ha'aretz

We thank You for this Land

Meditation

May You bring us to feasts and festivals in peace,
and may we celebrate them in joy in Your holy city,
Jerusalem.

    Nodeh l'kha: We thank You for the Land of Israel.

Ritual

On the eve or day of Yom Ha'atzma'ut, invite friends and family to a *seudat mitzvah*, a festive meal, that features produce, food products, flowers, and wines that are grown or made in Israel. Serve foods representing Israel's pluralist fusion of culinary traditions and play traditional and contemporary music by Israeli composers and performers. When you invite your guests, ask them to bring an object that reflects their relationship to Israel. Examples might be a *tallit* or *kiddush* cup bought in Israel, a certificate for trees planted in Israel, *Hadassah* or *Jerusalem Report* magazines, family photographs taken at Masada, a passport stamped at Ben Gurion Airport. The object needn't come from Israel; it could be a newspaper article. After you arrange all the objects on a ceremonial plate, ask the guests to tell the story of how their objects represent the blessings and challenges Israel poses.

Blessing

We ask Your blessings…for the State of Israel, for the Land of Israel, and for the people of Israel…. May we be among those who faithfully resolve to encourage, to strengthen, and to support the Land, its people, and its heritage.

(Likrat Shabbat)

Culminate your celebration by offering personal blessings for Israel that have emerged from the stories your objects evoked. You might begin a personal blessing this way:

יברכך

Yevarekh'ekha _____.

May you, Israel, be blessed with _____.

(Complete the blessing with your own words and hopes.)

Teaching

May God bless you from Zion. May you see
Jerusalem prosper all the days of your life.... May
there be peace for the people Israel.

(Adapted from Psalms 128)

Rabbi Hiyya bar Ashi quoted Rav: In the time to
come, all the wild trees of the Land of Israel will
bear fruit, for it is written in the Torah: "For the
trees have borne their fruit; fig trees and vines have
yielded their strength."

(Babylonian Talmud: Ketubot 112b)

HOLY DAYS
Shavuot

STUDYING TOGETHER ON SHAVUOT

If we say "We were slaves in Egypt" during Passover, shouldn't we be saying "We were free at the foot of Mount Sinai" on Shavuot? For on Shavuot, we celebrate the moment when we stood at Sinai and became a people. Just as the Passover seder allows us to experience the movement from slavery to free- dom, studying together with Jews from diverse communities on the eve of Shavuot allows us to reen- act the time we all stood at Sinai. In sacred conver- sation, we chal- lenge each other to see our ancient text anew. We cel- ebrate our unity by asking the questions we can't answer alone.

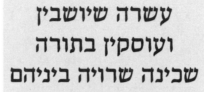

עשרה שיושבין
ועוסקין בתורה
שכינה שרויה ביניהם

*Asarah she'yoshvin
v'oskin ba'Torah
Shekhinah sheruyah
beinei'hem*

When ten people study
Torah together, the Divine
Presence hovers over them

Meditation

One God,
One people,
One mountain,
One book.
Many voices.

Hinei mah tov
How good it is:
One people, together.

Ritual

Step 1: Invite friends of diverse Jewish backgrounds to study together on Shavuot. (This traditional evening of Torah study that lasts all night is called a *tikkun leil Shavuot*. Many communities hold a *tikkun* on the first night of Shavuot, ending with morning prayers at sunrise. You might choose to hold a special communitywide Jewish study event in preparation for Shavuot.)

Step 2: Consider the text in "Teaching" as a starting point for discussion. In a small group, or with a partner, read aloud this description of the experience at Sinai.

Step 3: Ask each other: How do we relate our lives to this text? It may help to recall a moment in your own life when you "tasted" or fully understood a deep truth. What happened? What did you understand? How did this moment change you? Share your responses in your conversations.

Step 4: At Sinai, we had an experience that was both personal and shared. Ask as part of your conversation: How do our contemporary stories unify us? What, on their deepest level, do our experiences have in common?

Blessing

(Before you study)

ברוך אתה ה' אלקינו מלך העולם
אשר קדשנו במצותיו וצונו לעסוק בדברי תורה.

*Barukh atah Adonai eloheinu melekh ha'olam asher
kidshanu b'mitzvotav v'tzivanu la'asok b'divrei Torah.*

Praised are You, Source of All, who makes our
lives holy through *mitzvot* and calls us to study Torah together.

Teaching

When the Holy One spoke, each and every person
in Israel could say, "The Divine Word is addressing
me." Rabbi Yosi, the son of Hanina, said: Do not be
surprised by this idea. For when manna came
down to feed Israel, each person tasted it according
to his or her capacity. For infants it was like mother's milk, for the young it was like bread with oil
and honey, and for the old like a honey cracker.
What is true about the manna is also true about the
Divine Word. Therefore the Holy One said: "Do not
be misled if you hear many voices. Know that I am
the One God for each of you."

(Pesikta de Rav Kahana *12:25*)

HOLY DAYS
Rosh Chodesh

CELEBRATING ROSH CHODESH

Rosh Chodesh, when a sliver of moon appears in the sky marking the beginning of a new month, is a time of celebration. The stars can be seen the most clearly, and we articulate our wishes for the coming month. In the past twenty years, Rosh Chodesh has been reclaimed by Jewish women as a time for reflection, healing, and celebration.

חודש טוב!

Chodesh tov!

Have a good month!

Meditation

May the New Moon bring new possibilities for life, for healing, and for celebration.

Ritual

Allow the events and images of the past month to run through your mind. From the many memories, choose two that you wish to take with you into the next month. Remember something you learned from them.

Imagine being cleansed of all that was difficult during the past month, letting go of anger and disappointment. Would it be possible to forgive yourself for what you failed to accomplish and for what you were not yet able to be?

Alone or, better yet, with friends or family, light a candle on the eve of the New Moon, taking the time you need to look deeply into the flame, time to become centered and renewed. You might light an ordinary candle, a wick floating in oil over water, or a long-burning candle. Celebrate the New Moon with study, music, and good food.

Blessing
(Lighting a candle)

Blessed are You who gives us the New Moon,

A sign of beginning anew.

Blessed are You,

As we start all over again.

As the New Moon becomes visible as the month of _____
begins, let it be a month of joy, hope, vision, and renewal.

Teaching

God makes the moon to mark the seasons;

The sun knows when to set.

You bring on darkness and it is night,

When all the beasts in the forest stir.

(Psalms 104:19–20)

The women heard about the construction of the
Golden Calf and refused to submit their jewelry
to their husbands. Instead they said to them, "Do
you want to construct an idol that has no power
to redeem us? We will not listen to you." And the
Holy One rewarded them in this world in that they
would go out to observe the New Moons more than
men, and in the world to come they will be
renewed like the New Moons.

(Pirkei d'Rabbi Eliezer 45)

Our Rosh Chodesh group began as a group of women gathering to support a friend who was saying *kaddish* for her daughter. Since then, we have marked many life-passages together, both joyous and sad: adopting children, divorce, watching our sons and daughters become *b'nei mitzvah*, and now becoming grandmothers. We are woven together by the rituals, old and new, that we have done over the past thirteen years.

(Dr. Shoshana Silberman)

ABOUT THE
TRANSLATIONS

Translations and adaptations of biblical sources are based on
*Tanakh: A New Translation of the Holy Scriptures, According to the
Traditional Hebrew Text*, The Jewish Publication Society, 1985.

ABOUT CLAL

CLAL—The National Jewish Center for Learning and Leadership was founded in 1974. A think tank, leadership training institute and resource center, CLAL convenes interdisciplinary conversations that explore the Jewish and American futures, and enhances Jewish participation in civic and spiritual life in North America. Its faculty includes rabbis from every denomination and scholars from a broad array of disciplines, including anthropology, political science, and philosophy. CLAL combines Jewish texts and intellectual traditions with cutting-edge contemporary scholarship in its work to transform Jewish communities around the country.

CLAL'S MISSION

CLAL's mission is to:

- Stimulate volunteer, professional and rabbinic leadership to build responsive Jewish communities across North America.

- Help individuals to imagine new Jewish possibilities.

- Promote inclusive Jewish communities in which all voices are heard.

- Convene interdisciplinary conversations that explore the Jewish and American futures.

- Enhance Jewish participation in civic and spiritual life in North America.

For further information, please contact CLAL, 440 Park Avenue South, 4th floor, New York, New York 10016; Tel: (212) 779-3300; Fax: (212) 779-1009; www.clal.org.

Notes

Notes

About JEWISH LIGHTS Publishing

People of all faiths and backgrounds yearn for books that attract, engage, educate and spiritually inspire.

Our principal goal is to stimulate thought and help all people learn about who the Jewish People are, where they come from, and what the future can be made to hold. While people of our diverse Jewish heritage are the primary audience, our books speak to people in the Christian world as well and will broaden their understanding of Judaism and the roots of their own faith.

We bring to you authors who are at the forefront of spiritual thought and experience. While each has something different to say, they all say it in a voice that you can hear.

Our books are designed to welcome you and then to engage, stimulate and inspire. We judge our success not only by whether or not our books are beautiful and commercially successful, but by whether or not they make a difference in your life.

We at Jewish Lights take great care to produce beautiful books that present meaningful spiritual content in a form that reflects the art of making high quality books. Therefore, we want to acknowledge those who contributed to the production of this book.

Stuart M. Matlins

Stuart M. Matlins, Publisher

PRODUCTION
Tim Holtz & Bridgett Taylor

EDITORIAL
Amanda Dupuis, Martha McKinney,
Polly Short Mahoney & Emily Wichland

COVER DESIGN
Stacey Hood, Big EyeDea Visual Design, Waitsfield, Vermont

TEXT DESIGN & TYPESETTING
Peter Bertolami, Graphic Identity, Brookfield, Connecticut

JACKET / TEXT PRINTING & BINDING
Transcontinental Printing, Peterborough, Ontario

Spirituality

Does the Soul Survive?
A Jewish Journey to Belief in Afterlife, Past Lives & Living with Purpose
by *Rabbi Elie Kaplan Spitz*; Foreword by *Brian L. Weiss, M.D.*

Spitz relates his own experiences and those shared with him by people he has worked with as a rabbi, and shows us that belief in afterlife and past lives, so often approached with reluctance, is in fact true to Jewish tradition. 6 x 9, 288 pp, HC, ISBN 1-58023-094-6 **$21.95**

The Women's Torah Commentary: *New Insights from Women Rabbis on the 54 Weekly Torah Portions* Ed. by *Rabbi Elyse Goldstein*

For the first time, women rabbis provide a commentary on the entire Torah. In a week-by-week format; a perfect gift for others, or for yourself.
6 x 9, 496 pp, HC, ISBN 1-58023-076-8 **$34.95**

The Gift of Kabbalah
Discovering the Secrets of Heaven, Renewing Your Life on Earth
by *Tamar Frankiel, Ph.D.*

Makes accessible the mysteries of Kabbalah. Traces Kabbalah's evolution in Judaism and shows us its most important gift: a way of revealing the connection between our "everyday" life and the spiritual oneness of the universe. 6 x 9, 256 pp, HC, ISBN 1-58023-108-X **$21.95**

Bringing the Psalms to Life: *How to Understand and Use the Book of Psalms*
by Rabbi Daniel F. Polish 6 x 9, 208 pp, Quality PB, ISBN 1-58023-157-8 **$16.95**;
HC, ISBN 1-58023-077-6 **$21.95**

The Empty Chair: *Finding Hope and Joy—*
Timeless Wisdom from a Hasidic Master, Rebbe Nachman of Breslov AWARD WINNER!
4 x 6, 128 pp, Deluxe PB, 2-color text, ISBN 1-879045-67-2 **$9.95**

The Gentle Weapon: *Prayers for Everyday and Not-So-Everyday Moments*
Adapted from the Wisdom of Rebbe Nachman of Breslov
4 x 6, 144 pp, Deluxe PB, 2-color text, ISBN 1-58023-022-9 **$9.95**

Ancient Secrets: *Using the Stories of the Bible to Improve Our Everyday Lives*
by Rabbi Levi Meier, Ph.D. 5½ x 8½, 288 pp, Quality PB, ISBN 1-58023-064-4 **$16.95**

Or phone, fax, mail or e-mail to: **JEWISH LIGHTS** Publishing
Sunset Farm Offices, Route 4 • P.O. Box 237 • Woodstock, Vermont 05091
Tel: (802) 457-4000 • Fax: (802) 457-4004 • www.jewishlights.com
Credit card orders: **(800) 962-4544** (9AM–5PM ET Monday–Friday)
Generous discounts on quantity orders. SATISFACTION GUARANTEED. Prices subject to change.

Spirituality

My People's Prayer Book: *Traditional Prayers, Modern Commentaries*
Ed. by *Dr. Lawrence A. Hoffman*

Provides a diverse and exciting commentary to the traditional liturgy, helping modern men and women find new wisdom in Jewish prayer, and bring liturgy into their lives. Each book includes Hebrew text, modern translation, and commentaries *from all perspectives* of the Jewish world.
Vol. 1—*The Sh'ma and Its Blessings,* 7 x 10, 168 pp, HC, ISBN 1-879045-79-6 **$23.95**
Vol. 2—*The Amidah,* 7 x 10, 240 pp, HC, ISBN 1-879045-80-X **$23.95**
Vol. 3—*P'sukei D'zimrah* (Morning Psalms), 7 x 10, 240 pp, HC, ISBN 1-879045-81-8 **$24.95**
Vol. 4—*Seder K'riat Hatorah* (The Torah Service), 7 x 10, 264 pp, ISBN 1-879045-82-6 **$23.95**
Vol. 5—*Birkhot Hashachar* (Morning Blessings), 7 x 10, 256 pp, ISBN 1-879045-83-4 **$24.95**

Becoming a Congregation of Learners
Learning as a Key to Revitalizing Congregational Life by Isa Aron, Ph.D.;
Foreword by Rabbi Lawrence A. Hoffman, Co-Developer, Synagogue 2000
6 x 9, 304 pp, Quality PB, ISBN 1-58023-089-X **$19.95**

Self, Struggle & Change
Family Conflict Stories in Genesis and Their Healing Insights for Our Lives
by Dr. Norman J. Cohen 6 x 9, 224 pp, Quality PB, ISBN 1-879045-66-4 **$16.95**;
HC, ISBN 1-879045-19-2 **$21.95**

Voices from Genesis: *Guiding Us through the Stages of Life*
by Dr. Norman J. Cohen 6 x 9, 192 pp, Quality PB, ISBN 1-58023-118-7 **$16.95**;
HC, ISBN 1-879045-75-3 **$21.95**

God Whispers: *Stories of the Soul, Lessons of the Heart*
by Rabbi Karyn D. Kedar 6 x 9, 176 pp, Quality PB, ISBN 1-58023-088-1 **$15.95**

The Business Bible: *10 New Commandments for Bringing Spirituality & Ethical Values into the Workplace*
by Rabbi Wayne Dosick 5½ x 8½, 208 pp, Quality PB, ISBN 1-58023-101-2 **$14.95**

Being God's Partner: *How to Find the Hidden Link Between Spirituality and Your Work*
by Rabbi Jeffrey K. Salkin; Intro. by Norman Lear AWARD WINNER!
6 x 9, 192 pp, Quality PB, ISBN 1-879045-65-6 **$16.95**; HC, ISBN 1-879045-37-0 **$19.95**

God & the Big Bang
Discovering Harmony Between Science & Spirituality AWARD WINNER!
by Daniel C. Matt 6 x 9, 224 pp, Quality PB, ISBN 1-879045-89-3 **$16.95**

Soul Judaism: *Dancing with God into a New Era*
by Rabbi Wayne Dosick 5½ x 8½, 304 pp, Quality PB, ISBN 1-58023-053-9 **$16.95**

Finding Joy: *A Practical Spiritual Guide to Happiness* AWARD WINNER!
by Rabbi Dannel I. Schwartz with Mark Hass
6 x 9, 192 pp, Quality PB, ISBN 1-58023-009-1 **$14.95**; HC, ISBN 1-879045-53-2 **$19.95**

Theology/Philosophy

Love and Terror in the God Encounter: *The Theological Legacy of Rabbi Joseph B. Soloveitchik, Vol. 1*   by *Dr. David Hartman*

Renowned scholar David Hartman explores the sometimes surprising intersection of Soloveitchik's rootedness in halakhic tradition with his genuine responsiveness to modern Western theology. An engaging look at one of the most important Jewish thinkers of the twentieth century. 6 x 9, 240 pp, HC, ISBN 1-58023-112-8 **$25.00**

These Are the Words: *A Vocabulary of Jewish Spiritual Life*

by *Arthur Green*

What are the most essential ideas, concepts and terms that an educated person needs to know about Judaism? From *Adonai* (My Lord) to *zekhut* (merit), this enlightening and entertaining journey through Judaism teaches us the 149 core Hebrew words that constitute the basic vocabulary of Jewish spiritual life. 6 x 9, 304 pp, Quality PB, ISBN 1-58023-107-1 **$18.95**

Broken Tablets: *Restoring the Ten Commandments and Ourselves*

Ed. by *Rabbi Rachel S. Mikva;* Intro. by *Rabbi Lawrence Kushner*   AWARD WINNER!

Twelve outstanding spiritual leaders each share profound and personal thoughts about these biblical commands and why they have such a special hold on us.
6 x 9, 192 pp, HC, ISBN 1-58023-066-0 **$21.95**

A Heart of Many Rooms: *Celebrating the Many Voices within Judaism*   AWARD WINNER!
by Dr. David Hartman   6 x 9, 352 pp, HC, ISBN 1-58023-048-2 **$24.95**

A Living Covenant: *The Innovative Spirit in Traditional Judaism*   AWARD WINNER!
by Dr. David Hartman   6 x 9, 368 pp, Quality PB, ISBN 1-58023-011-3 **$18.95**

Evolving Halakhah: *A Progressive Approach to Traditional Jewish Law*
by Rabbi Dr. Moshe Zemer   6 x 9, 480 pp, HC, ISBN 1-58023-002-4 **$40.00**

The Death of Death: *Resurrection and Immortality in Jewish Thought*   AWARD WINNER!
by Dr. Neil Gillman   6 x 9, 336 pp, Quality PB, ISBN 1-58023-081-4 **$18.95**

The Last Trial: *On the Legends and Lore of the Command to Abraham to Offer Isaac as a Sacrifice*   by Shalom Spiegel   6 x 9, 208 pp, Quality PB, ISBN 1-879045-29-X **$17.95**

Tormented Master: *The Life and Spiritual Quest of Rabbi Nahman of Bratslav*
by Dr. Arthur Green   6 x 9, 416 pp, Quality PB, ISBN 1-879045-11-7 **$18.95**

The Earth Is the Lord's: *The Inner World of the Jew in Eastern Europe*
by Abraham Joshua Heschel   5½ x 8, 128 pp, Quality PB, ISBN 1-879045-42-7 **$14.95**

A Passion for Truth: *Despair and Hope in Hasidism*   by Abraham Joshua Heschel
5½ x 8, 352 pp, Quality PB, ISBN 1-879045-41-9 **$18.95**

Your Word Is Fire: *The Hasidic Masters on Contemplative Prayer*   Ed. by Dr. Arthur Green and Dr. Barry W. Holtz   6 x 9, 160 pp, Quality PB, ISBN 1-879045-25-7 **$14.95**

Healing/Wellness/Recovery

Jewish Paths toward Healing and Wholeness
A Personal Guide to Dealing with Suffering
by *Rabbi Kerry M. Olitzky;* Foreword by *Debbie Friedman*

Why me? Why do we suffer? How can we heal? Grounded in personal experience with illness and Jewish spiritual traditions, this book provides healing rituals, psalms and prayers that help readers initiate a dialogue with God, to guide them along the complicated path of healing and wholeness. 6 x 9, 192 pp, Quality PB, ISBN 1-58023-068-7 **$15.95**

Healing of Soul, Healing of Body
Spiritual Leaders Unfold the Strength & Solace in Psalms
Ed. by *Rabbi Simkha Y. Weintraub, CSW,* for The National Center for Jewish Healing

A source of solace for those who are facing illness, as well as those who care for them. Provides a wellspring of strength with inspiring introductions and commentaries by eminent spiritual leaders reflecting all Jewish movements.
6 x 9, 128 pp, Quality PB, Illus., 2-color text, ISBN 1-879045-31-1 **$14.95**

Jewish Pastoral Care
A Practical Handbook from Traditional and Contemporary Sources
Ed. by *Rabbi Dayle A. Friedman*

Gives today's Jewish pastoral counselors practical guidelines based in the Jewish tradition.
6 x 9, 464 pp, HC, ISBN 1-58023-078-4 **$35.00**

Twelve Jewish Steps to Recovery: *A Personal Guide to Turning from Alcoholism &* *Other Addictions . . . Drugs, Food, Gambling, Sex . . .* by Rabbi Kerry M. Olitzky & Stuart A. Copans, M.D. Preface by Abraham J. Twerski, M.D.; Intro. by Rabbi Sheldon Zimmerman; "Getting Help" by JACS Foundation 6 x 9, 144 pp, Quality PB, ISBN 1-879045-09-5 **$13.95**

One Hundred Blessings Every Day: *Daily Twelve Step Recovery Affirmations,* *Exercises for Personal Growth & Renewal Reflecting Seasons of the Jewish Year* by Rabbi Kerry M. Olitzky 4½ x 6½, 432 pp, Quality PB, ISBN 1-879045-30-3 **$14.95**

Recovery from Codependence: *A Jewish Twelve Steps Guide to Healing Your Soul* by Rabbi Kerry M. Olitzky 6 x 9, 160 pp, Quality PB, ISBN 1-879045-32-X **$13.95**; HC, ISBN 1-879045-27-3 **$21.95**

Renewed Each Day: *Daily Twelve Step Recovery Meditations Based on the Bible* by Rabbi Kerry M. Olitzky & Aaron Z. Vol. I: *Genesis & Exodus;* Vol. II: *Leviticus,* *Numbers and Deuteronomy*
Vol. I: 6 x 9, 224 pp, Quality PB, ISBN 1-879045-12-5 **$14.95**
Vol. II: 6 x 9, 280 pp, Quality PB, ISBN 1-879045-13-3 **$14.95**

Life Cycle/Grief

Against the Dying of the Light
A Parent's Story of Love, Loss and Hope
by *Leonard Fein*

The sudden death of a child. A personal tragedy beyond description. Rage and despair deeper than sorrow. What can come from it? Raw wisdom and defiant hope. In this unusual exploration of heartbreak and healing, Fein chronicles the sudden death of his 30-year-old daughter and reveals what the progression of grief can teach each one of us.
5½ x 8½, 176 pp, HC, ISBN 1-58023-110-1 **$19.95**

Mourning & Mitzvah, 2nd Ed.: *A Guided Journal for Walking the Mourner's Path through Grief to Healing* with *Over 60 Guided Exercises*
by *Anne Brener, L.C.S.W.*

For those who mourn a death, for those who would help them, for those who face a loss of any kind, Brener teaches us the power and strength available to us in the fully experienced mourning process. Revised and expanded. 7½ x 9, 304 pp, Quality PB, ISBN 1-58023-113-6 **$19.95**

Grief in Our Seasons: *A Mourner's Kaddish Companion*
by *Rabbi Kerry M. Olitzky*

A wise and inspiring selection of sacred Jewish writings and a simple, powerful ancient ritual for mourners to read each day, to help hold the memory of their loved ones in their hearts. Offers a comforting, step-by-step daily link to saying Kaddish.
4½ x 6½, 448 pp, Quality PB, ISBN 1-879045-55-9 **$15.95**

Tears of Sorrow, Seeds of Hope
A Jewish Spiritual Companion for Infertility and Pregnancy Loss
by Rabbi Nina Beth Cardin   6 x 9, 192 pp, HC, ISBN 1-58023-017-2 **$19.95**

A Time to Mourn, A Time to Comfort
A Guide to Jewish Bereavement and Comfort
by Dr. Ron Wolfson   7 x 9, 336 pp, Quality PB, ISBN 1-879045-96-6 **$18.95**

When a Grandparent Dies
A Kid's Own Remembering Workbook for Dealing with Shiva and the Year Beyond
by Nechama Liss-Levinson, Ph.D.
8 x 10, 48 pp, HC, Illus., 2-color text, ISBN 1-879045-44-3 **$15.95**

Spirituality/Jewish Meditation

Discovering Jewish Meditation
Instruction & Guidance for Learning an Ancient Spiritual Practice
by *Nan Fink Gefen*

Gives readers of any level of understanding the tools to learn the practice of Jewish meditation on your own, starting you on the path to a deep spiritual and personal connection to God and to greater insight about your life. 6 x 9, 208 pp, Quality PB, ISBN 1-58023-067-9 **$16.95**

Entering the Temple of Dreams: *Jewish Prayers, Movements, and Meditations for the End of the Day* by *Tamar Frankiel* and *Judy Greenfeld*

Nighttime spirituality is much more than bedtime prayers! Here, you'll uncover deeper meaning to familiar nighttime prayers—and learn to combine the prayers with movements and meditations to enhance your physical and psychological well-being.
7 x 10, 192 pp, Quality PB, Illus., ISBN 1-58023-079-2 **$16.95**

One God Clapping: *The Spiritual Path of a Zen Rabbi* Award Winner!
by *Alan Lew* with *Sherril Jaffe*

A fascinating personal story of a Jewish meditation expert's roundabout spiritual journey from Zen Buddhist practitioner to rabbi. 5½ x 8½, 336 pp, Quality PB, ISBN 1-58023-115-2 **$16.95**

The Handbook of Jewish Meditation Practices
A Guide for Enriching the Sabbath and Other Days of Your Life
by *Rabbi David A. Cooper*

Gives us ancient and modern Jewish tools—Jewish practices and traditions, easy-to-use meditation exercises, and contemplative study of Jewish sacred texts. 6 x 9, 208 pp, Quality PB, ISBN 1-58023-102-0 **$16.95**

Stepping Stones to Jewish Spiritual Living: *Walking the Path Morning, Noon, and Night*
by Rabbi James L. Mirel & Karen Bonnell Werth
6 x 9, 240 pp, Quality PB, ISBN 1-58023-074-1 **$16.95**

Meditation from the Heart of Judaism
Today's Teachers Share Their Practices, Techniques, and Faith
Ed. by Avram Davis 6 x 9, 256 pp, Quality PB, ISBN 1-58023-049-0 **$16.95**;
HC, ISBN 1-879045-77-X **$21.95**

The Way of Flame: *A Guide to the Forgotten Mystical Tradition of Jewish Meditation*
by Avram Davis 4½ x 8, 176 pp, Quality PB, ISBN 1-58023-060-1 **$15.95**

Minding the Temple of the Soul: *Balancing Body, Mind, and Spirit through Traditional Jewish Prayer, Movement, and Meditation*
by Tamar Frankiel and Judy Greenfeld 7 x 10, 184 pp, Quality PB, Illus.,
ISBN 1-879045-64-8 **$16.95**; Audiotape of the Blessings and Meditations (60-min. cassette), JN01 **$9.95**; Videotape of the Movements and Meditations (46-min.), S507 **$20.00**

Children's Spirituality

God Said Amen
by *Sandy Eisenberg Sasso*
Full-color illus. by *Avi Katz*

For ages 4 & up

A warm and inspiring tale of two kingdoms: one overflowing with water but without oil to light its lamps; the other blessed with oil but no water to grow its gardens. The kingdoms' rulers ask God for help but are too stubborn to ask each other. It takes a minstrel, a pair of royal riding-birds and their young keepers, and a simple act of kindness to show that they need only reach out to each other to find God's answer to their prayers.

9 x 12, 32 pp, HC, Full-color illus., ISBN 1-58023-080-6 **$16.95**

For Heaven's Sake
by *Sandy Eisenberg Sasso*; Full-color illus. by *Kathryn Kunz Finney*

For ages 4 & up

Everyone talked about heaven: "Thank heavens." "Heaven forbid." "For heaven's sake, Isaiah." But no one would say what heaven was or how to find it. So Isaiah decides to find out, by seeking answers from many different people.
9 x 12, 32 pp, HC, Full-color illus., ISBN 1-58023-054-7 **$16.95**

But God Remembered
Stories of Women from Creation to the Promised Land

For ages 8 & up

by *Sandy Eisenberg Sasso*; Full-color illus. by *Bethanne Andersen*

A fascinating collection of four different stories of women only briefly mentioned in biblical tradition and religious texts. Vibrantly brings to life courageous and strong women from ancient tradition; all teach important values through their actions and faith.
9 x 12, 32 pp, HC, Full-color illus., ISBN 1-879045-43-5 **$16.95**

God in Between
by *Sandy Eisenberg Sasso*; Full-color illus. by *Sally Sweetland*

For ages 4 & up

If you wanted to find God, where would you look? A magical, mythical tale that teaches that God can be found where we are: within all of us and the relationships between us.
9 x 12, 32 pp, HC, Full-color illus., ISBN 1-879045-86-9 **$16.95**

For ages 4 & up

A Prayer for the Earth: The Story of Naamah, Noah's Wife
by *Sandy Eisenberg Sasso*; Full-color illus. by *Bethanne Andersen*

This new story, based on an ancient text, opens readers' religious imaginations to new ideas about the well-known story of the Flood. When God tells Noah to bring the animals of the world onto the ark, God also calls on Naamah, Noah's wife, to save each plant on Earth.
9 x 12, 32 pp, HC, Full-color illus., ISBN 1-879045-60-5 **$16.95**

Children's Spirituality

In Our Image
God's First Creatures

For ages
4 & up

by *Nancy Sohn Swartz*

Full-color illus. by *Melanie Hall*

A playful new twist on the Creation story—from the perspective of the animals. Celebrates the interconnectedness of nature and the harmony of all living things. "The vibrantly colored illustrations nearly leap off the page in this delightful interpretation." —*School Library Journal*

9 x 12, 32 pp, HC, Full-color illus., ISBN 1-879045-99-0 **$16.95**

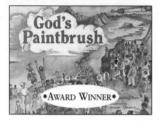
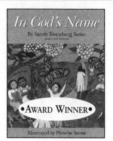

God's Paintbrush

For ages
4 & up

by *Sandy Eisenberg Sasso*; Full-color illus. by *Annette Compton*

Invites children of all faiths and backgrounds to encounter God openly in their own lives. Wonderfully interactive; provides questions adult and child can explore together at the end of each episode.

11 x 8½, 32 pp, HC, Full-color illus., ISBN 1-879045-22-2 **$16.95**

Also available: A Teacher's Guide: **A Guide for Jewish & Christian Educators and Parents**
8½ x 11, 32 pp, PB, ISBN 1-879045-57-5 **$8.95**

God's Paintbrush Celebration Kit 9½ x 12, HC, Includes 5 sessions/40 full-color Activity Sheets and Teacher Folder with complete instructions, ISBN 1-58023-050-4 **$21.95**

In God's Name

For ages
4 & up

by *Sandy Eisenberg Sasso*; Full-color illus. by *Phoebe Stone*

Like an ancient myth in its poetic text and vibrant illustrations, this award-winning modern fable about the search for God's name celebrates the diversity and, at the same time, the unity of all the people of the world.

9 x 12, 32 pp, HC, Full-color illus., ISBN 1-879045-26-5 **$16.95**

What Is God's Name? (A Board Book)

For ages
0–4

An abridged board book version of the award-winning *In God's Name.*

5 x 5, 24 pp, Board, Full-color illus., ISBN 1-893361-10-1 **$7.95** A SKYLIGHT PATHS Book

The 11th Commandment: Wisdom from Our Children

For
all ages

by *The Children of America*

"If there were an Eleventh Commandment, what would it be?" Children of many religious denominations across America answer this question—in their own drawings and words. "A rare book of spiritual celebration for all people, of all ages, for all time."—*Bookviews*

8 x 10, 48 pp, HC, Full-color illus., ISBN 1-879045-46-X **$16.95**

Children's Spirituality

Because Nothing Looks Like God
by *Lawrence and Karen Kushner*
Full-color illus. by *Dawn W. Majewski*

For ages
4 & up

MULTICULTURAL, NONDENOMINATIONAL, NONSECTARIAN
What is God like? The first collaborative work by husband-and-wife team Lawrence and Karen Kushner introduces children to the possibilities of spiritual life. Real-life examples of happiness and sadness—from goodnight stories, to the hope and fear felt the first time at bat, to the closing moments of life—invite us to explore, together with our children, the questions we all have about God, no matter what our age.

11 x 8½, 32 pp, HC, Full-color illus., ISBN 1-58023-092-X **$16.95**

Where Is God?
What Does God Look Like?
How Does God Make Things Happen? (Board Books)

For ages
0–4

by *Lawrence and Karen Kushner*; Full-color illus. by *Dawn W. Majewski*
Gently invites children to become aware of God's presence all around them. Three board books abridged from *Because Nothing Looks Like God* by Lawrence and Karen Kushner.
Each 5 x 5, 24 pp, Board, Full-color illus. **$7.95** SKYLIGHT PATHS Books

Sharing Blessings
Children's Stories for Exploring the Spirit of the Jewish Holidays
by *Rahel Musleah* and *Rabbi Michael Klayman*
Full-color illus. by *Mary O'Keefe Young*

For ages
6 & up

What is the spiritual message of each of the Jewish holidays? How do we teach it to our children? Many books tell children about the historical significance and customs of the holidays. Through stories about one family's preparation, *Sharing Blessings* explores ways to get into the *spirit* of 13 different holidays.
8½ x 11, 64 pp, HC, Full-color illus., ISBN 1-879045-71-0 **$18.95**

The Book of Miracles
A Young Person's Guide to Jewish Spiritual Awareness
by *Lawrence Kushner*

For ages
9 & up

Introduces kids to a way of everyday spiritual thinking to last a lifetime. Kushner, whose award-winning books have brought spirituality to life for countless adults, now shows young people how to use Judaism as a foundation on which to build their lives.
6 x 9, 96 pp, HC, 2-color illus., ISBN 1-879045-78-8 **$16.95**

Spirituality & More

The Jewish Lights Spirituality Handbook
A Guide to Understanding, Exploring & Living a Spiritual Life
Ed. by *Stuart M. Matlins, Editor-in-Chief, Jewish Lights Publishing*

Rich, creative material from over 50 spiritual leaders on every aspect of Jewish spirituality today: prayer, meditation, mysticism, study, rituals, special days, the everyday, and more.
6 x 9, 456 pp, Quality PB, ISBN 1-58023-093-8 **$18.95**; HC, ISBN 1-58023-100-4 **$24.95**

Six Jewish Spiritual Paths: *A Rationalist Looks at Spirituality*
by *Rabbi Rifat Sonsino*

The quest for spirituality is universal, but which path to spirituality is right *for you?* A straightforward, objective discussion of the many ways—each valid and authentic—for seekers to gain a richer spiritual life within Judaism. 6 x 9, 208 pp, HC, ISBN 1-58023-095-4 **$21.95**

Criminal Kabbalah
An Intriguing Anthology of Jewish Mystery & Detective Fiction
Edited by *Lawrence W. Raphael*; Foreword by *Laurie R. King*

Twelve of today's best known mystery authors provide an intriguing collection of new stories sure to enlighten at the same time they entertain.
6 x 9, 256 pp, Quality PB, ISBN 1-58023-109-8 **$16.95**

Mystery Midrash: *An Anthology of Jewish Mystery & Detective Fiction* Award Winner!
Ed. by Lawrence W. Raphael 6 x 9, 304 pp, Quality PB, ISBN 1-58023-055-5 **$16.95**

Sacred Intentions: *Daily Inspiration to Strengthen the Spirit, Based on Jewish Wisdom*
by Rabbi Kerry M. Olitzky & Rabbi Lori Forman
4½ x 6½, 448 pp, Quality PB, ISBN 1-58023-061-X **$15.95**

Restful Reflections: *Nighttime Inspiration to Calm the Soul, Based on Jewish Wisdom*
by Rabbi Kerry M. Olitzky & Rabbi Lori Forman
4½ x 6½, 448 pp, Quality PB, ISBN 1-58023-091-1 **$15.95**

The Enneagram and Kabbalah: *Reading Your Soul*
by Rabbi Howard A. Addison 6 x 9, 176 pp, Quality PB, ISBN 1-58023-001-6 **$15.95**

Embracing the Covenant: *Converts to Judaism Talk About Why & How*
Ed. and with Intros. by Rabbi Allan L. Berkowitz and Patti Moskovitz
6 x 9, 192 pp, Quality PB, ISBN 1-879045-50-8 **$15.95**

Wandering Stars: *An Anthology of Jewish Fantasy & Science Fiction* Ed. by Jack Dann; Intro. by Isaac Asimov 6 x 9, 272 pp, Quality PB, ISBN 1-58023-005-9 **$16.95**

Israel—A Spiritual Travel Guide Award Winner!
A Companion for the Modern Jewish Pilgrim
by Rabbi Lawrence A. Hoffman 4¾ x 10, 256 pp, Quality PB, ISBN 1-879045-56-7 **$18.95**

Spirituality—The Kushner Series
Books by Lawrence Kushner

The Way Into Jewish Mystical Tradition

Explains the principles of Jewish mystical thinking, their religious and spiritual significance, and how they relate to our lives. A book that allows us to experience and understand the Jewish mystical approach to our place in the world. 6 x 9, 224 pp, HC, ISBN 1-58023-029-6 **$21.95**

Eyes Remade for Wonder
The Way of Jewish Mysticism and Sacred Living

A Lawrence Kushner Reader Intro. by *Thomas Moore*

Whether you are new to Kushner or a devoted fan, you'll find inspiration here. With samplings from each of Kushner's works, and a generous amount of new material, this book is to be read and reread, each time discovering deeper layers of meaning in our lives.
6 x 9, 240 pp, Quality PB, ISBN 1-58023-042-3 **$16.95**; HC, ISBN 1-58023-014-8 **$23.95**

Because Nothing Looks Like God

by *Lawrence and Karen Kushner;* Full-color illus. by *Dawn W. Majewski*

What is God like? The first collaborative work by husband-and-wife team Lawrence and Karen Kushner introduces children to the possibilities of spiritual life with three poetic spiritual stories. Real-life examples of happiness and sadness—from goodnight stories, to the hope and fear felt the first time at bat, to the closing moments of life—invite us to explore, together with our children, the questions we all have about God, no matter what our age. **For ages 4 & up**
11 x 8½, 32 pp, HC, Full-color illus., ISBN 1-58023-092-X **$16.95**

Invisible Lines of Connection: *Sacred Stories of the Ordinary* AWARD WINNER!
6 x 9, 160 pp, Quality PB, ISBN 1-879045-98-2 **$15.95**; HC, ISBN 1-879045-52-4 **$21.95**

Honey from the Rock: *An Introduction to Jewish Mysticism* SPECIAL ANNIVERSARY EDITION
6 x 9, 176 pp, Quality PB, ISBN 1-58023-073-3 **$15.95**

The Book of Letters: *A Mystical Hebrew Alphabet* AWARD WINNER!
Popular HC Edition, 6 x 9, 80 pp, 2-color text, ISBN 1-879045-00-1 **$24.95**; *Deluxe Gift Edition,* 9 x 12, 80 pp, HC, 2-color text, ornamentation, slipcase, ISBN 1-879045-01-X **$79.95**; *Collector's Limited Edition,* 9 x 12, 80 pp, HC, gold-embossed pages, hand-assembled slipcase. With silkscreened print. Limited to 500 signed and numbered copies, ISBN 1-879045-04-4 **$349.00**

The Book of Words: *Talking Spiritual Life, Living Spiritual Talk* AWARD WINNER!
6 x 9, 160 pp, Quality PB, 2-color text, ISBN 1-58023-020-2 **$16.95**;
152 pp, HC, ISBN 1-879045-35-4 **$21.95**

God Was in This Place & I, i Did Not Know
Finding Self, Spirituality and Ultimate Meaning
6 x 9, 192 pp, Quality PB, ISBN 1-879045-33-8 **$16.95**

The River of Light: *Jewish Mystical Awareness* SPECIAL ANNIVERSARY EDITION
6 x 9, 192 pp, Quality PB, ISBN 1-58023-096-2 **$16.95**

Women's Spirituality / Ecology

Torah of the Earth: *Exploring 4,000 Years of Ecology in Jewish Thought*
In 2 Volumes   Ed. by *Rabbi Arthur Waskow*

Major new resource offering us an invaluable key to understanding the intersection of ecology and Judaism. Leading scholars provide us with a guided tour of ecological thought from four major Jewish viewpoints.
Vol. 1: *Biblical Israel & Rabbinic Judaism*, 6 x 9, 272 pp, Quality PB, ISBN 1-58023-086-5 **$19.95**
Vol. 2: *Zionism & Eco-Judaism*, 6 x 9, 336 pp, Quality PB, ISBN 1-58023-087-3 **$19.95**

Ecology & the Jewish Spirit: *Where Nature & the Sacred Meet* Ed. and with Intros.
by Ellen Bernstein 6 x 9, 288 pp, Quality PB, ISBN 1-58023-082-2 **$16.95**;
HC, ISBN 1-879045-88-5 **$23.95**

The Jewish Gardening Cookbook: *Growing Plants & Cooking for Holidays & Festivals*
by Michael Brown 6 x 9, 224 pp, Illus., Quality PB, ISBN 1-58023-116-0 **$16.95**;
HC, ISBN 1-58023-004-0 **$21.95**

Moonbeams: *A Hadassah Rosh Hodesh Guide*

Ed. by *Carol Diament, Ph.D.*

This hands-on "idea book" focuses on *Rosh Hodesh*, the festival of the new moon, as a source of spiritual growth for Jewish women. A complete sourcebook that will initiate or rejuvenate women's study groups, it is also perfect for women preparing for *bat mitzvah*, or for anyone interested in learning more about *Rosh Hodesh* observance and what it has to offer. 8½ x 11, 240 pp, Quality PB, ISBN 1-58023-099-7 **$20.00**

The Women's Torah Commentary: *New Insights from Women Rabbis on the 54 Weekly Torah Portions* Ed. by *Rabbi Elyse Goldstein*

For the first time, women rabbis provide a commentary on the entire Five Books of Moses. More than 25 years after the first woman was ordained a rabbi in America, these inspiring teachers bring their rich perspectives to bear on the biblical text. In a week-by-week format; a perfect gift for others, or for yourself. 6 x 9, 496 pp, HC, ISBN 1-58023-076-8 **$34.95**

Lifecycles, in Two Volumes   AWARD WINNERS!
V. 1: *Jewish Women on Life Passages & Personal Milestones*
Ed. and with Intros. by Rabbi Debra Orenstein
V. 2: *Jewish Women on Biblical Themes in Contemporary Life*
Ed. and with Intros. by Rabbi Debra Orenstein and Rabbi Jane Rachel Litman
V. 1: 6 x 9, 480 pp, Quality PB, ISBN 1-58023-018-0 **$19.95**; HC, ISBN 1-879045-14-1 **$24.95**
V. 2: 6 x 9, 464 pp, Quality PB, ISBN 1-58023-019-9 **$19.95**

ReVisions: *Seeing Torah through a Feminist Lens* AWARD WINNER!
by Rabbi Elyse Goldstein 5½ x 8½, 224 pp, Quality PB, ISBN 1-58023-117-9 **$16.95**;
208 pp, HC, ISBN 1-58023-047-4 **$19.95**

The Year Mom Got Religion: *One Woman's Midlife Journey into Judaism*
by Lee Meyerhoff Hendler 6 x 9, 208 pp, Quality PB, ISBN 1-58023-070-9 **$15.95**

Life Cycle & Holidays

How to Be a Perfect Stranger, 2nd Ed. In 2 Volumes
A Guide to Etiquette in Other People's Religious Ceremonies
Ed. by *Stuart M. Matlins* & *Arthur J. Magida*   **AWARD WINNER!**

What will happen? What do I do? What do I wear? What do I say? What are their basic beliefs? Should I bring a gift? Explains the rituals and celebrations of North America's major religions/denominations, helping an interested guest to feel comfortable. *Not* presented from the perspective of any particular faith. SKYLIGHT PATHS Books
Vol. 1: *North America's Largest Faiths,* 6 x 9, 432 pp, Quality PB, ISBN 1-893361-01-2 **$19.95**
Vol. 2: *Other Faiths in North America,* 6 x 9, 416 pp, Quality PB, ISBN 1-893361-02-0 **$19.95**

Celebrating Your New Jewish Daughter
Creating Jewish Ways to Welcome Baby Girls into the Covenant— New and Traditional Ceremonies
by *Debra Nussbaum Cohen;* Foreword by *Rabbi Sandy Eisenberg Sasso*

Features everything families need to plan a celebration that reflects Jewish tradition, including a how-to guide to new and traditional ceremonies, and practical guidelines for planning the joyous event. 6 x 9, 272 pp, Quality PB, ISBN 1-58023-090-3 **$18.95**

The New Jewish Baby Book   **AWARD WINNER!**
Names, Ceremonies & Customs—A Guide for Today's Families
by Anita Diamant 6 x 9, 336 pp, Quality PB, ISBN 1-879045-28-1 **$18.95**

Parenting As a Spiritual Journey
Deepening Ordinary & Extraordinary Events into Sacred Occasions
by Rabbi Nancy Fuchs-Kreimer 6 x 9, 224 pp, Quality PB, ISBN 1-58023-016-4 **$16.95**

Putting God on the Guest List, 2nd Ed.   **AWARD WINNER!**
How to Reclaim the Spiritual Meaning of Your Child's Bar or Bat Mitzvah
by Rabbi Jeffrey K. Salkin 6 x 9, 224 pp, Quality PB, ISBN 1-879045-59-1 **$16.95**

For Kids—Putting God on Your Guest List
How to Claim the Spiritual Meaning of Your Bar or Bat Mitzvah
by Rabbi Jeffrey K. Salkin 6 x 9, 144 pp, Quality PB, ISBN 1-58023-015-6 **$14.95**

Bar/Bat Mitzvah Basics, 2nd Ed.: *A Practical Family Guide to Coming of Age Together*
Ed. by Cantor Helen Leneman 6 x 9, 240 pp, Quality PB, ISBN 1-58023-151-9 **$18.95**

Hanukkah, 2nd Ed.: The Family Guide to Spiritual Celebration
by Dr. Ron Wolfson 7 x 9, 192 pp, Quality PB, Illus., ISBN 1-58023-122-5 **$18.95**

The Shabbat Seder: The Art of Jewish Living
by Dr. Ron Wolfson 7 x 9, 272 pp, Quality PB, Illus., ISBN 1-879045-90-7 **$16.95**

The Passover Seder: The Art of Jewish Living
by Dr. Ron Wolfson 7 x 9, 352 pp, Quality PB, Illus., ISBN 1-879045-93-1 **$16.95**